— P

Why Are You Still ⌐ ⌐ ⌐ g ⌐ ⌐ ⌐ ⌐ ⌐ ⌐ ⌐ ⌐ ⌐

This amazing book will give you the courage to think seriously about giving your child a more authentic, playful, and joyful learning journey. It cracked my imagination wide open and convinced me that something radically different is not only possible, it's necessary. Everything you need to create a better future for your child, by making every day better right now, is inside these pages.

—JANE McGONIGAL, *New York Times* bestselling author of *Reality is Broken: Why Games Make Us Better and How They Can Change the World*

Blake Boles is back with another provocative challenge to parents and guardians. If mainstream schooling isn't working for your child, maybe it's time to consider the alternatives. Yes, your kids can still go to college, And, yes, they can have a conventionally successful career. However, once families step out of the traditional education box, they never know where the path might lead.

—DANIEL H. PINK, *New York Times* bestselling author of *Drive, When,* and *A Whole New Mind*

A thoughtful, powerful look at the generous act of trusting your kids enough to let them find their own educational rhythm. School and learning are different, and what we need for our future is a focus on more learning and less test-taking.

—SETH GODIN, author of *Stop Stealing Dreams*

There is so much goodness in this powerful, game-changing book! The message (like the title) is bold, and yet Blake's writing is always thoughtful and nuanced. He offers heaps of friendly guidance and lays out the relevant research with clarity and discernment. Without stooping to hyperbole or manipulation, Blake will have parents wondering why, indeed, they are still sending their kids to school. Better yet, he'll help them drop unnecessary stress and worry—and help their kids find meaningful, engaged, and joyful paths through life.

—GRACE LLEWELLYN, author of
The Teenage Liberation Handbook

This book will push you, provoke you, and quite possibly inspire you to rethink every core assumption you hold about education. Be prepared to open your eyes to radically different ways of preparing kids for radically different forms of "success."

—TED DINTERSMITH, author of *What School Could Be* and producer of *Most Likely to Succeed*

Kids don't need school; they need space to explore and time to think. This book will show you how to give your kids a real education by encouraging them to discover their interests instead of merely following someone else's directions.

—PENELOPE TRUNK, serial entrepreneur
and writer @ penelopetrunk.com

Blake Boles offers a stimulating and important perspective on improving the well-being of young people everywhere.

—JOHANN HARI, *New York Times* bestselling author
of *Chasing the Scream* and *Lost Connections*

Blake's new book is a major contribution to the growing understanding of Self-Directed Education. It addresses, straight on, in thoughtful, respectful, and compelling ways the major concerns parents have when they think about the possibility of this approach to education for their children. If you care about children and the future, read this!

—PETER GRAY, Research Professor at Boston College and author of *Free to Learn*

Blake poses the $64,000 question and then draws a detailed roadmap for parents to follow, replete with testimonials from self-directed students, the researchers who have followed them, and the educators who have witnessed their journeys.

—PAT MONTGOMERY, founder of the Clonlara School and author of *The School That's Inside You*

Blake's book is one I wish I had had on my shelf when I was leading my five kids to adulthood. He thoughtfully leads us to consider our preconceptions, beliefs, and aspirations and then gives us a buffet of options that can be paired with a particular teenager—rather than following culturally-derived, one-size-fits-all ideas about education and employment. I especially appreciated how he showed that young people can "signal" a readiness for employment with or without college. A great read and a must-have for the parents of teens.

—JULIE BOGART, author of *The Brave Learner*

WHY
ARE YOU STILL
SENDING YOUR KIDS TO
SCHOOL?

BLAKE BOLES

WHY ARE YOU STILL SENDING YOUR KIDS TO SCHOOL?

the case for helping them leave,

chart their own paths,

and prepare for adulthood at

their own pace

BLAKE BOLES

TELLS PEAK PRESS

Published in the United States by Tells Peak Press, Loon Lake, CA

Cover and interior design by Zoe Norvell (zoenorvell.com)

First edition

ISBN: 978-0-9860119-7-9

E-book ISBN: 978-0-9860119-8-6

Library of Congress Control Number: 2020904729

For bulk orders and other inquiries, visit blakeboles.com

Table of Contents

An Invitation to Connect

Over the years, readers have filled my inbox with kind notes, illuminating stories, and friendly challenges to my ideas—all of which I appreciate.

If something in this book calls to you, I invite you to reach out. Find me at blakeboles.com.

Furthermore: if you have a project, venture, or wild idea that might benefit from my involvement, I'm all ears. Collaborations are the stuff of life.

INTRODUCTION

Where We'll Go in This Book

What do you do if school isn't a good fit for your child?

Some kids just don't mesh with school in big, obvious ways: they're viciously bullied or repeatedly harassed. They're threatened with suspension. They battle you over homework every night.

Other kids suffer in less visible ways. They sit, bored out of their minds, hour after hour, week after week. They spiral quietly into depression. They start using legal or illegal substances to make it through the day.

What do you do when you see your child's spark fading? What do you do when you witness a creeping anxiety in the brave child you once knew? What do you do when you run out of reasonable explanations for this continued suffering?

People are complex. You may never figure out exactly why school stopped working for your kid, but you *can* reasonably assume that school—not your kid—is a large part of the problem.

This is not a book about how to reform the education system. While that subject is vitally important, reform is not something for which you can afford to wait. Nor is this a book that argues for tearing down public schools, which provide certain essential services to our society and genuinely work for some kids.

This is a practical book about what you can do, beginning

today, if you believe that mainstream schools, which I call conventional schools, may be a bad fit for your child.

Attention is a precious resource, and you may be wondering if this book is worth your time. Allow me to provide a brief tour of the ideas and arguments you'll encounter in the pages ahead.

In this Introduction, I first address the issue of privilege, explain how conventional schooling transformed into an institution that can harm kids, and introduce some of my colleagues in the hope that you will not write me off as an isolated crank.

In Chapter 1, I take you on a tour of the wide world of radical alternatives to school. It's an incredibly exciting time to be an outside-the-box learner in North America where we enjoy a thriving ecosystem of alternatives: private and public, school-based and home-based. This ecosystem is so dynamic, in fact, that it sometimes feels like the Wild West. Some alternatives might inspire you, while others could send you screaming in the opposite direction. Some cities and towns are packed with great options, while others are deserts. Homeschooling will occupy much of our discussion; I'll encourage you to think of it as a handy meta-tool instead of a specific method of educating (i.e., doing school at home). Homeschooling is a legal, viable option in all 50 states of the U.S., in all 10 provinces of Canada, as well as in the United Kingdom, Australia, New Zealand, and some European countries. If you live outside these areas, your situation might be trickier, but the large-scale trend is undoubtedly positive. Today you enjoy more options for thriving outside of conventional school than ever before.

In Chapter 2, I acknowledge the reality that for many jobs today, your kid *will* need a college degree—which is why it's important to know that unconventional educational paths can lead to college admissions and gainful employment. Fortunately, thousands have walked this path before, and the news is good: if a non-traditionally educated young person wants to go to college, she can go to college. If she wants to work in a certain field, she can work in that field. Her timeline may look different. She may need to play catch-up. She may attend community college while her peers are still in high school. Fundamentally, however, she will not face any closed doors.

Even with such promises, a big concern remains for many parents: if I don't force my kid to work hard today, how will they learn to work hard tomorrow? That's our focus in Chapter 3, where we'll dip into the realms of anthropology and psychology to see how (and why) self-directed young people voluntarily challenge themselves, gain important knowledge, and otherwise function in the adult world, even when it seems like they're just hanging out all day. I also offer concrete suggestions for engaging adolescents in real world adventures.

The paths described in this book aren't "life hacks" for achieving the same ends as conventional education, i.e., maximizing your kid's social status and earning potential. While some unconventionally educated young people do end up in high-prestige and high-paying careers, many do not. Alternative education is a broadly middle-class phenomenon that leads to broadly middle-class outcomes. If your non-negotiable desire is to maximize the number of upper-case letters after your kid's name or the number of zeroes in their paycheck, my book won't help you. It *will* help you support your kid's journey toward a meaningful career and more genuine relationships—including their relationship with you.

The parent-child relationship is our focus in Chapter 4, in which we investigate the phenomenon of intensive parenting: the widely accepted dogma of modern child-rearing. Intensive parenting claims that parents can finely control their children's destinies through goal-oriented molding, shaping, and nudging. With the help of a rogue scholar named Judith Rich Harris, we'll dismantle this belief by examining the relative power of genes, environment, and peer groups. Ultimately, I'll recommend that you stop thinking of yourself as the manager of your kid's education and start seeing yourself as their consultant: someone who gives advice, shares expertise, and provides resources while remaining fundamentally detached from the specific outcomes of this process. Countless parents have told me that giving up this amount of control is a scary but vitally necessary step for building the kind of relationship they want to have with their kid.

Stepping away from intensive parenting is difficult, of course, when everyone around you seems to be grooming their kid for college admissions, whether that kid is in eighth grade, in preschool, or in utero. That's why we question the necessity of four-year college in Chapter 5, looking closely at the wonderful things that we assume to happen there. For whom specifically do these wonderful things happen? How can we think clearly about the pros and cons of the many paths to and through higher education? I make the case that you can afford to relax about when your kid goes to college, where they go to college, or whether they go to college at all. Which means you can afford to relax about parenting, which in turn means you can afford to relax about supporting your kid's alternative educational path—the one that clearly serves them right now. Which, ultimately, is the point of this book.

Finally, in Chapter 6, we zoom out to focus on young people's mental health and sense of connection. If your kid wins in the game of school but finds himself miserable, disconnected, and unable to get off the proverbial hamster wheel, then have you succeeded in parenting and education? Economic security is important, but it is not everything. Help your kids connect to what matters most in our world. That's what counts, and that's all you can do. Everything else is gravy.

A Note About Privilege

If you visit an unconventional school or a homeschooling conference in North America, I'll tell you right now: you're entering a world that's largely represented by white, middle-class, and two-college-graduate families. Alternative education is dominated by those with enough security to play around with innovative and unproven educational paths, and perhaps it always will be. This is the nature of "alternative."

This fact makes some parents feel uncomfortable, especially liberal parents who feel simultaneously aligned with the individualist principles of child-centered education and the collectivist mission of public education.

I encourage you to not give up immediately if this world rubs you the wrong way. Go beyond surface appearances and you'll see that there are no "Keep Out" signs posted here. The many alternative schools, self-directed learning centers, and homeschooling communities I've visited are not little country clubs designed to shelter their children from their less privileged peers. That's the private school stereotype. While most alternatives described in this book are, in fact, private (i.e., they don't receive any government funding), they're also overwhelmingly welcoming, inclusive, and increasingly diverse.

While not yet representative of the United States as a whole, there is a sizable and growing number of low-income families, people of color, and young people with disabilities in the alternative education world. Take a moment to read Jessica Huseman's article in *The Atlantic*, "The Rise of Homeschooling Among Black Families." Look online for talks by Sugata Mitra and Akilah Richards. Find Luba Vangelova's reporting on the self-directed learning communities serving underprivileged kids in Chicago, Thailand, and India. (I provide links in the "Notes" that follow this chapter.) Google the Albany Free School, Brooklyn Free School, Philadelphia Free School, Natural Creativity Center, and Lighthouse Holyoke. Some self-directed learning centers in Georgia and North Carolina already possess a majority of non-white enrollees and staff. Less privileged folks have always found ways to help their children thrive despite mind-boggling obstacles, and today is no different.

If the thought of pulling your kid out of public school still makes you feel guilty, you're not alone. Some critics argue that choosing to homeschool means depriving your child's less-privileged classmates of the test-score-boosting "peer effects" that your (presumably more privileged) kid brings to school. Other critics suggest that conventional schools are the best, and only, way for children to gain an appreciation of racial and socioeconomic diversity—and therefore opting out of the system is tantamount to feeding a separatist movement. Finally, if you or your kid is a member of a minority group that was historically denied access to the public education system, some suggest that it's virtually treasonous to not remain a loyal member of that system.

I'm the first to admit that alternative education can't work for everyone, as the common criticism goes. Kids with severe disabilities, kids with uninvolved or overextended parents, and kids who are recent immigrants, to name only a few examples, almost certainly need lots of support, which may be found most easily and cheaply in a well-resourced public school. The public education system evolved to serve a critical child welfare function in our society—one that should not be discarded.

Even if alternative education doesn't work for everyone in an absolute sense, it does work for a surprising number of cases. A child with multiple special needs living in a rural area may be better served by a caring homeschooling community than a poorly equipped public system. A small alternative school may effectively mitigate the racial discrimination or sense of segregation that your child feels in a large conventional school.

If you can take one of the paths described in this book, then by all means, acknowledge your luck and privilege, but don't get bogged down with guilt. Accessibility isn't worth much if what you access hurts your child. Education and schooling are not the same thing, and you owe no loyalty to schools that do little educating.

Why Do Schools Exist?

Now you know where we're going, but where are we coming from? Since this book positions itself in opposition to conventional school, I'd like to put my biases on the table and explain why I believe conventional schools exist, how they emerged, and whom they ultimately serve. (Feel free to skip ahead to Chapter 1 if you'd like to get to the practical stuff.)

Formal schooling has existed in every modern civilization, but until recently it occupied only a minuscule fraction of children's lives. Early schools were typically religious, just for boys, and focused on the three R's (reading, writing, and arithmetic). Even in 1852, when the state of Massachusetts instituted the United States' first compulsory schooling law, children ages 8 to 14 were required to attend just 12 weeks per year.

School in its modern incarnation, as the full-time occupation of every child until at least age 16, emerged only in the second half of the nineteenth century when the idea of mass-schooling gained popularity across the world thanks to its success in Prussia. In the United States, large waves of European immigrants fueled the rapid growth of state schools for the purpose of assimilating and homogenizing the (predominantly Catholic) newcomers who were landing on (predominantly Protestant) American shores.

At the same moment in history, popular opinion was turning against the idea of children working 12-hour days in dark, satanic mills (as William Blake called them). Schools became the conscionable alternative to full-time child labor in factories, farms, and home enterprises. Conveniently, these new schools would save kids from exploitation while also preventing them from competing with adults for a limited pool of jobs—an especially attractive prospect in the aftermath of a worldwide depression.

Idle hands are the devil's tools, and schools served double duty as devices for getting kids off the streets and keeping them out of trouble. But now that all the kids were rounded up, what would we do with them? Thus emerged our national system of secondary schools and the idea of universal academic training: an idea that extended far beyond school's historical mission of teaching reading, writing, and arithmetic. From 1910 to 1960, high school enrollment rose from 10% to 90% in the United States, and high school graduation rates leapt from 5% to 65%. In just half a century, secondary education transformed from a rarity into a commonplace experience.

By the 1970s, the mass-schooling project was complete. With few exceptions, children in developed nations around the world attended school until at least age 16. Compulsory education became a hallmark of progress. Children everywhere now followed broad-based academic curricula that were supposed to expand their minds, prepare them for an increasingly knowledge- and service-oriented economy, and assimilate them into a common citizenship.

The expansion of schooling that took place between the mid-nineteenth and mid-twentieth centuries marked nothing less than a revolution in how humanity viewed its younger members. The primary occupation of kids permanently shifted from laboring to learning. A child's purpose was no longer to support her family, but rather to succeed in a system of full-time, academics-centered, age-segregated, and expert-managed schooling.

Just a hundred years ago, your child may have been working long shifts in a coal mine, cannery, textile factory, or performing repetitive labor on your farm or in your home-based business. Most families were relatively poor in those days, which is why you may have resisted sending your kid to school (as many parents did); it represented a threat to your family's economic security.

Thankfully, most children living in developed nations today don't need to take grueling, mindless jobs in order to help their families escape poverty. Economic development is largely responsible for this miracle, but schools also played an important role, and they undoubtedly deserve some credit for improving the day-to-day experiences of children across the world.

Now I'd like you to consider a less comfortable hypothesis.

While schools once performed the valuable role of rescuing kids from life in the factories or on the streets, I believe they have gradually ceded the moral high ground. Like a soaked bathtub sponge toy, schools have swollen to incredible proportions, far beyond their original intent and scope. Like a hostile nation, they have invaded and conquered children's lives (and they probably dictate large swaths of your life as a parent, too). They make impossible demands of their students, fill their lives with inane tasks, and pit them against each other in competition for fabricated rewards. School began as an institution that rescued young people from degrading labor. Now schools are the perpetuators of degrading labor.

How could this be true? Consider that the threat of

exploitative child labor has departed from the shores of our economically developed nation, perhaps forever. Those dark, satanic mills have either been outsourced to foreign lands, or they have evolved into clean, well-lit, and highly mechanized factories. Modern-day captains of industry aren't rubbing their sweaty palms, awaiting the collapse of school so they may once again employ pliable 10-year-olds; they're desperately seeking competent adults who can design and run their expensive computers and automated machinery.

We have reached a unique moment in history, one in which children have been rendered economically useless. Young people once had the mandate and capacity to contribute to the economy; now we charge them with the vague mission of "getting educated." Yet so much of modern-day education is an elaborate game of job market signaling (a phenomenon we'll investigate closely in Chapter 5). Little substantive learning, challenge, and growth takes place in modern schools, and to the extent that these good things do happen, they may have happened incidentally without school.

Students suspect that school is a sham. Many teachers and administrators suspect that it's a sham (although it's in their interest not to admit it). If you're reading this book, then I suspect that you, too, suspect that it's a sham. Yet we all keep playing the conventional school game, because we don't know what other game there is to play, and we don't know what to do with kids who can't really contribute to our economy.

The most practical function of modern schooling is to give children a safe place to exist while their parents work. A less flattering way to say this is that school is free childcare.

Mirroring the rise of modern welfare states, schools have become social service providers for the marginalized and underprivileged. From the point of view of child welfare, this is clearly a positive development. For many kids today, school is the one place where they'll reliably find a warm meal, caring adults, and a respite from physical danger.[1]

Yet we must be careful to distinguish between the childcare, welfare, and molding functions of school. Only some families rely on school as a social service provider, while virtually all parents rely on school to keep their kids off the streets and out of the house. Most parents don't know what happens at school, and many don't care as long as it keeps their kids safely occupied.

At their best, perhaps we can think of conventional schools as well-resourced libraries, staffed with friendly social workers. At their worst, schools are more akin to prisons or mental institutions—holding chambers that separate kids from the adult world where they have no place.

For far too many, schools are places where kids are forced to do things that don't really matter, exclusively for the benefit of adults, when they could be doing something better with their time. In this way, schools are the new child labor.

If schools embraced their fundamental roles as childcare and social service providers, offered personalized instruction in the three R's (which virtually everyone agrees is of value), and made their other offerings optional, then perhaps they wouldn't be so bad. But that's not how schools currently function. Our schools intellectually force-feed their students.

---

1 We're ignoring the possibility of school shootings and routine school violence, of course.

They test and measure and assess *ad nauseam*, far beyond any utility such testing might offer. We tell ourselves that school is created with children's best interests in mind, but how can we be sure of that when the interests of school so closely align with the interests of adults?

Schools employ millions of adults and fuel billion-dollar textbook industries. Schools are places where adults feel powerful and deserving of respect, but not because they earned it; their clients have been coerced into attendance and cannot represent their own interests. No one likes being overtly managed and controlled, no matter their age.

If school were made voluntary, how many kids would participate? Sure, many would still use school as a place to meet friends, get a free lunch, and sometimes seek an adult's help. Sure, young people would still worry about their economic futures. But how many of them would happily enroll in the full-time school project, replete with classes, tests, grades, and homework?

Idle hands are the devil's tools, indeed, yet it is our hands that are idle: the parents, educators, administrators, textbook makers, educational service providers, and everyone else feeding the chimera of mass-schooling. Over the past century we have built up a fantastically profitable schooling industry even as the moral basis of schooling—protecting children from exploitative labor—has evaporated.

C.S. Lewis wrote that "Of all tyrannies, a tyranny sincerely exercised for the good of its victims may be the most oppressive." For many children, school is a genuinely tyrannical experience. If you're reading this book, your own child has probably experienced some version of that tyranny. And for every parent like you—someone with the time, resources, and courage to explore alternative paths—there are a dozen others whose children suffer in parallel. The mission of this book is to help you muster the courage and martial the resources necessary to escape this tyranny, and in doing so, inspire others to do the same.

Fellow Travelers

If this is your first time reading a book that broadly criticizes conventional schooling, you may be feeling a bit defensive right now. School as an oppressive institution? School as the new child labor? If you succeeded in the conventional school system, I understand that I may be testing your patience. But before you toss this book into the fireplace, I implore you to stick around just a little longer and hear from the other voices of the alternative education movement. I am not, in fact, an isolated crank.

Below I share a few of the powerful voices I've encountered in this world and a taste of their writings. The alternative education world, despite being small and scrappy, possesses an intellectual vitality that's deserving of respect.

John Taylor Gatto taught in New York City public schools for nearly 30 years, won multiple awards (including New York State Teacher of the Year twice in a row), and then quit his job to write and speak about the harm that he and other well-intentioned educators inflicted upon the children they were meant to serve. Gatto holds a special place in my heart because he was my gateway into the world of unconventional education. He also penned the best single definition of education that I've ever found:

> Whatever an education is, it should make you a unique individual, not a conformist; it should furnish you with an original spirit with which to tackle the big challenges; it should allow you to find values which will be your roadmap through life; it should make you spiritually rich, a person who loves whatever you are doing, wherever you are, whomever you are with; it should teach you what is important, how to live and how to die.

To start your foray into Gatto territory, search online for his essay, "The Seven-Lesson Schoolteacher", and then proceed to his books *A Different Kind of Teacher* and *Dumbing Us Down*.

Grace Llewellyn wrote her timeless treatise, *The Teenage Liberation Handbook*, with frustrated adolescents in mind as her audience, but the book has inspired countless parents as well. The first line of Chapter 1 caught me, hook, line, and sinker, way back at age 21: "How strange and self-defeating that a supposedly free country should train its young for life in totalitarianism." Llewellyn also compiled a book about the lives of African American homeschoolers (*Freedom Challenge*) and founded Not Back to School Camp, the summer camp for teens who don't attend conventional school, where I've worked for more than a decade. The third and final edition of the *Teenage Liberation Handbook* —for which I serve as editor—is coming soon.

Peter Gray, the Boston College research professor who you'll encounter many times in the pages ahead, is the founder of The Alliance for Self-Directed Education and the author of a popular *Psychology Today* blog. In his excellent book, *Free to Learn*, Gray names the seven sins of forced education:

1. Denial of liberty without just cause and due process
2. Interference with the development of personal responsibility and self-direction
3. Undermining of intrinsic motivation to learn (turning learning into work)
4. Judging students in ways that foster shame, hubris, cynicism, and cheating
5. Interference with the development of cooperation and promotion of bullying
6. Inhibition of critical thinking
7. Reduction in diversity of skills and knowledge

Carol Black's online essays, which criticize modern systems of education, are works of art that should be hung in galleries. Begin with "A Thousand Rivers," where Black describes what the modern world has forgotten about children and learning:

> When you see children who do not learn well in school, they will often display characteristics that would be valued and admired if they lived in any number of traditional societies around the world. They are physically energetic; they are independent; they are sociable; they are funny. They like to do things with their hands. They crave real play, play that is exuberant, that tests their strength and skill and daring and endurance; they crave real work, work that is important, that is concrete, that makes a valued contribution. They dislike abstraction; they dislike being sedentary; they dislike authoritarian control. They like to focus on the things that interest them, that spark their curiosity, that drive them to tinker and explore. [. . .] Watch your child's

eyes, what makes them go dull and dead, what makes them
brighten, quicken, glow with light. That is where learning lies.

John Holt, father of the unschooling movement,
wrote a number of highly influential books including *How
Children Fail, How Children Learn*, and *Teach Your Own*, but
I recommend starting with his brief essay from 1969, "School
is Bad for Children." Read it and ask yourself how much
things have changed in half a century:

Our compulsory school-attendance laws once served
a humane and useful purpose. They protected the children's
right to some schooling, against those adults who would
otherwise have denied it to them in order to exploit their
labor, in farm, store, mine or factory. Today the laws help
nobody - not the schools, not the teachers, not the children. To keep kids in school who would rather not be there
costs the schools an enormous amount of time and trouble - to say nothing of what it costs to repair the damage
that these angry and resentful prisoners do every time they
get a chance. Every teacher knows that any kid in class
who, for whatever reason, would rather not be there, not
only doesn't learn anything himself but makes it a great
deal tougher for anyone else. As for protecting the children
from exploitation, the chief and indeed only exploiters of
children these days are the schools.

Alfie Kohn offers a powerful voice for parents who
are just starting to dip their toes into alternative thinking.
His classic books include *Punished by Rewards* and *Unconditional Parenting*, but you can start with his online essays,
where you'll find wit and wisdom such as this:

> Don't let anyone tell you that standardized tests are not accurate measures. The truth of the matter is they offer a remarkably precise method for gauging the size of the houses near the school where the test was administered.

Finally, **Ned Johnson** and **William Stixrud** wrote *The Self-Driven Child*, another great book for parents who are just getting started in this world. Though the authors don't directly condone the practices of conventional schools, they implicate them at every turn:

> Lest you doubt how little control children and adolescents [actually] have, think of what their days are like: they have to sit still in classes they didn't choose, taught by teachers randomly assigned to them, alongside whatever child happens to be assigned to their class. They have to stand in neat lines, eat on a schedule, and rely on the whims of their teachers for permission to go to the bathroom . . . It is frustrating and stressful to feel powerless, and many kids feel that way all the time.

If you "did fine" in school, you may feel reluctant to explore the voices listed above; they threaten a sense of accomplishment to which many of us (myself included) attached ourselves long ago. But investing just a few hours in these authors might pay lifelong dividends. It certainly did for me. Halfway through a degree in astrophysics at UC Berkeley in 2003, with vague plans to become a high school science teacher, a friend handed me a John Taylor Gatto book that beckoned me down the rabbit hole. Before I knew it, I was crafting my own degree in alternative education so I could focus on this work full-time. After graduating I played with different ways of working with young people outside the classroom, eventually starting my own little travel company for self-directed teenagers, Unschool Adventures, that served double duty as a research lab for me to learn about the lives of young people who follow unconventional paths. By my last count, I had spent roughly 20,000 hours working with young people in non-traditional educational environments over a 15-year period.

A few good books can bend the arc of one's life. It may feel uncomfortable to read criticism of the formal education system that we're all supposed to agree is good, but I hope that you'll sit with that discomfort, at least for a little while. If my voice doesn't resonate with you, I invite you to explore the others in our rich choir.

We, the Barbarians

For almost a thousand years, the Chinese practiced foot-binding: the purposeful disfiguring of women's feet in the name of beauty and status. By the nineteenth century, half of all the women in China—and virtually all high-status women—had their feet painfully bound as children.

For the vast majority of history, people considered same-sex marriage unthinkable. Only at the dawn of the twenty-first century did the tides turn: a fact we'll consider quaint—and perhaps a tad barbaric—at the dawn of the twenty-second century.

What will our descendants look back upon as the cruel and senseless acts of our era? This question has fascinated me ever since I was a child, mostly for its ego-crushing implications: no matter how enlightened we may consider ourselves, we are undoubtedly committing atrocities today that future generations will judge harshly.

In his book *The Honor Code*, the philosopher Kwame Anthony Appiah proposed that four modern practices will make future generations cringe: the prison system, the industrial meat system, the institutionalized and isolated elderly, and the degradation of the environment.

I agree with Appiah's assessment, but I believe he's missing a major contender: conventional schooling. I believe that future generations will look back at how education was practiced in the twentieth and early twenty-first centuries, shake their heads, and think to themselves, "How quaint and tragic. What barbarians we were."

Moral revolutions don't happen quickly. Powerful arguments against foot-binding existed for centuries in China before reform took place. In the modern era, we've had powerful arguments against child trafficking and genital mutilation for quite a long time—but only now are those horrors beginning to leave the historical stage. Tradition and convenience keep despicable practices alive long after their moral foundations have eroded.

The life of a modern student is clearly superior to that of so many children in the past. I don't believe that today's education system will be seen in the same light as factory farming or child trafficking. But we are nonetheless perpetuating a system that does serious harm to many young people. We may not be binding their feet, but we are binding their minds. Conventional schools fritter away large parts of children's lives, largely for the benefit of adults, and largely because we simply don't know what else to do.

Despite all its heft and momentum, I believe that modern conventional schooling is on its way out. In the future, there will be many accepted ways of education that don't involve such a colossal waste of human potential. Conventional schools may still exist, but if your kids don't mesh with them, your friends and family will no longer assume that your kids have failed to appropriately conform. Instead they'll ask you, "Why are you still sending your kids to school?"

Fortunately, for an ever-growing number of families, that future is already here. If your local school doesn't fit your kids' needs, you can do something radically different, and your kids will turn out fine in terms of their economic security, mental health, and functionality in society.

Walking an alternative educational path today requires courage, self-awareness, and yes, a certain degree of privilege. But the accessibility of such paths is only increasing. No matter where in the world you live, you're living in the best time ever to opt out of conventional school.

Now let's get started.

Notes

In the "Notes" section at the end of each chapter, you'll find the sources for my research and quotes. If you're not able to locate a specific source, feel free to reach out to me: https://blakeboles.com

For practical resources related to this chapter—and every other chapter in the book—please visit the book's dedicated webpage: https://blakeboles.com/y/

A Note About Privilege

"The Rise of Homeschooling Among Black Families" by Jessica Huseman (February 17, 2015). https://www.theatlantic.com/education/archive/2015/02/the-rise-of-homeschooling-among-black-families/385543/

"Can Self-Directed Learning Work for Underprivileged Children?" by Luba Vangelova (April 24, 2015). https://www.kqed.org/mindshift/40184/can-self-directed-learning-work-for-underprivileged-children

For some common arguments in favor of keeping your (presumably privileged) kid in public school, see "Liberals, Don't Homeschool Your Kids" by Dana Goldstein (February 16, 2012). https://slate.com/human-interest/2012/02/homeschooling-and-unschooling-among-liberals-and-progressives.html

The self-directed learning centers in Georgia and North Carolina, with a majority (or very significant representation) of non-white enrollees and staff include, as of January 2020, Heartwood Agile Learning Center (https://www.heartwoodalc.org/), Anna Julia Cooper Learning & Liberation Center (http://www.learningandliberation.org/), and Gastonia Freedom School (http://gastoniafreedom.org/).

Why Do Schools Exist?

On the broad connections between child labor, labor at home, and the rise of compulsory schooling, see Chapter 1 of *Homeschooling* by James G. Dwyer and Shawn F. Peters (2019).

Critics have compared schools to prisons and mental institutions for a long time. In 1968, for example, Philip Jackson discussed this in his book *Life in Classrooms*: "There is an important fact about a student's life that teachers and parents often prefer not to talk about, at least not in front of students. This is the fact that young people have to be in school, whether they want to be or not. In this regard students have something in common with the members of two other of our social institutions that have involuntary attendance: prisons and mental hospitals. The analogy, though dramatic, is not intended to be shocking, and certainly there is no comparison between the unpleasantness of life for inmates of our prisons and mental institutions, on the other hand, and the daily travails of a first or second grader, on the other. Yet the school child, like the incarcerated adult, is, in a sense, a prisoner."

For statistics on high school enrollment and graduation rates in the twentieth century, see "How America Graduated From High School: 1910 to 1960" by Claudia Goldin (1994). https://dash.harvard.edu/handle/1/32785054

On the idea of school as a holding chamber for children while their parents work, see "Public School is a Babysitting Service" by Penelope Trunk (September 17, 2012). http://education.penelopetrunk.com/2012/09/17/public-school-is-a-babysitting-service

On the idea of school as the new child labor, see "How Homeschooling Fits in the Historical Narrative of Childhood" by Penelope Trunk (May 17, 2016). http://education.penelopetrunk.com/2016/05/17/how-homeschooling-fits-in-the-historical-narrative-of-childhood/. Also see psychologist Robert Epstein's comment cited in *Unschooled* by Kerry McDonald (2019): "A century ago, we rescued young people from the factories and the streets; now we need to rescue them from the schools."

Fellow Travelers

John Taylor Gatto's definition of education is from his book, *Dumbing Us Down* (2017).

Alfie Kohn's quote is from his essay "Fighting the Tests" (January 2001). https://www.alfiekohn.org/article/fighting-the-tests/

John Holt's essay, "School is Bad for Children," was originally published in his book *The Underachieving School* (1969).

We, the Barbarians

For more on moral revolutions and our cruel (but accepted) modern practices, see Kwame Anthony Appiah's book, *The Honor Code (2010).*

1: HIGH-QUALITY ALTERNATIVES EXIST

A Few Brief Stories

Kim Chin-Gibbons, age 13, suffered from a sleep disorder that caused her to miss school regularly. She barely passed eighth grade. "The pressures of school were constantly troubling my life," Kim told me. "I was always exhausted, sleeping my days away, and the homework would just keep piling up no matter what I did." Despite being a dedicated student, Kim felt indifferent about school. "I had passions, like music and reading for fun, that felt more beneficial for my happiness than schoolwork, but there was just no time."

Two weeks after starting ninth grade, Kim and her parents decided that she would never be happy there. Together, they decided that she should quit.

Tom Ochwat enjoyed a brief, happy year of Montessori preschool before he started attending Chicago public schools. "I absolutely hated it," Tom recalls. "Even though I was in all the gifted classes, I was bored with the material." He was light-years beyond his peers in math, and even though the school's staff attempted to accommodate him, they could never fulfill his need for accelerated learning.

In high school, Tom's boredom made a new friend—stress—that came from his lack of control over the school environment. "I'm the type of student who, if a teacher did something I disagreed with, would make my opinion known.

Public school doesn't deal with that very well." The pressures mounted, and in his sophomore year, Tom had to leave school to be hospitalized for clinical depression and anxiety.

Tom returned optimistic, but that feeling didn't last long. "After months of therapy, I hoped I would be able to handle my junior year. But not long into it, I knew I had to leave."

Gavin Lake of Omaha, Nebraska was one of those kids who could always get by in school despite the fact that almost none of the work interested him. "I just felt I had better things to do."

He breezed through elementary school, but in middle school, his grades started to dip. "My parents and I would fight every night over what I needed to do better. I just didn't care about school." In his first year of high school Gavin discovered filmmaking. "I loved it; I was good at it; and I wanted it to be my life." But between classes, homework, and everyday life, there was virtually no time left over for making movies.

Vanessa Reyes went to public school in Charlotte, North Carolina from kindergarten through third grade. "I felt like I had no power," Vanessa said at age 12. "I never did anything besides school, so I didn't have hobbies. I just hated it."

Vanessa's mom, Olivia, saw an anxious, rebellious, bored, and emotionally unregulated 9-year-old returning home each day from school. On one hand, she thought, maybe this is just what Vanessa is going through. It's normal to hate school. On the other hand, what if this isn't how it's supposed to be? What if school is damaging my daughter, and by continuing to send her there, I'm complicit?

Olivia began searching for alternatives.

Defining Conventionality

Do you know a Kim, Tom, Gavin, or Vanessa?

At some point, school rubs every kid the wrong way. For some of these kids, the friction is temporary: one bad teacher, one disruptive peer group, one dramatic episode with friends, or one challenging subject. (I'm looking at you, algebra.)

"Next year will be better," you gently advise. And it is.

For other kids, the conflict with school runs deep. It's not just a temporary ailment, it's an infection gone septic. For kids like these, time is not a healing balm; another day spent in school is truly a day wasted. For kids like these, school is not a liberating experience; it's a prison sentence.[2]

When school isn't working, we instinctively blame the students—they're too unmotivated, unfocused, social, hormonal, coddled, unruly, hyper, lazy, or stupid. When we've exhausted that line of reasoning, we blame the teachers and administrators—they're too lazy, selfish, unenlightened, unprepared, rigid, or bureaucratic.

But what if the problem doesn't lie with any individual? What if the problem lies with the entire way that we assume schooling must happen?

The hallmarks of a conventional school include:

- Mandatory curriculum
- Mandatory standardized testing
- Mandatory homework
- Narrow age grouping
- Grades

---

2 This isn't an extreme analogy, considering that many adolescents enjoy fewer personal freedoms than inmates or members of the armed services.

- Traditional power hierarchy (i.e., little voice for students)
- Little freedom for physical movement
- Little autonomy for teachers
- Little privacy for students
- Closed campus (e.g., no leaving school unless part of a supervised field trip)
- Specific arrival and departure hours

The more of these features a school has, the more conventional it is.

Does your kid's school have a no-homework policy? Does the school day start at 9:30 a.m. instead of 8:00 a.m.? Does it have an innovative new approach to grading? Does the student government have some real pull with the administration? Do the teachers enjoy a high degree of freedom to design their classes? Is there an extended recess or a generous number of field trips? Can you opt out of state tests? Yes? Wonderful. I say this without a hint of snark. These are victories worth celebrating. Still, in all likelihood, your kid's school remains highly conventional.

Conventionality runs deep in the education system, even in the schools that most people consider progressive or innovative.

Grace Llewellyn began her teaching career as a substitute in the late 1980s, where she quickly became disillusioned by the rigidity and dullness of public schools. She daydreamed about finding a "humane and lively" private school, and to her delight, she landed a job teaching middle school English at a small, independent school in Colorado. As she wrote in *The Teenage Liberation Handbook*, her colleagues were "flexible, enthusiastic, imaginative, intelligent, funny, and warm," and her classroom had only 19 students. It was a dream come true! Yet soon she realized something:

> ...this small, "caring," "creative" school was fundamentally the same as any ordinary public school, because it controlled students' lives. It continually dictated to them how to use their time. So what if they were role playing the lives of the early colonists instead of just reading the dry words of their American history textbook? These cute "experiential" activities we teachers took pride in had the same effect any schoolwork does. They stole kids' time and energy, so that John- the-math-genius-and-artist had no time to build his geometric sculptures, so that Andy couldn't pursue his fascination with well-made knives and guns, so that Kris and Chris and Rick and Young didn't have enough time to read, so that Shira—a brilliant actress and talented musician—was threatened with having to drop out of her outstanding chorale group if she missed any homework assignments.

Grace didn't want to make a hasty decision, so she stuck it out for a second year. Little changed. Then one day, while reading Henry David Thoreau's "On the Duty of Civil Disobedience" with her class, she discovered Thoreau's advice for public officials during the slave era: "If you really wish to do anything, resign your office." She resolved to quit teaching at the end of the school year.

Legions of educators, parents, and young people have made Grace's unhappy discovery: even when schools claim to be progressive or student-centered, most are fundamentally controlling places. What does it matter if a school down-plays grades, has a nice selection of electives, or gives students a flexible hour to work on personal projects each week? For those young people who refuse to be unfairly corralled, sub-dued, brow-beaten, or medicated, such things are band-aids on a spurting arterial wound.

How quickly we forget what it's like to be powerless in school. Some people love college enough to go back for a master's degree, but no one ever goes back to K–12 to relive those days. Consider the experience of a pediatric occupa-tional therapist who spent a single day observing her kid's middle school in 2014:

> I've been sitting for the past 90 excruciating minutes. I look down at my leg and notice it is bouncing. Great, I think to myself, now I'm fidgeting! I'm doing anything I can to pay attention—even contorting my body into awkward positions to keep from daydreaming. It is useless; I checked out about forty-five minutes ago. I'm no longer registering anything the teacher is saying. . .There is no way I could tolerate six hours of sitting even just one day, never mind every day – day after day. How on Earth do these children tolerate sitting this long?[3]

It's not just the kids who are powerless; the teachers have their hands tied, too. A former math teacher from Ontario, Canada, reported this in 2017:

---

3 Brian Huskie, a high school English teacher, has a tongue-in-cheek suggestion for helping adults to realize how mind-numbing school can be: require that all adults, on their 30th birthday, return to high school for four weeks.

The hardest thing to teach is mathematics. Not so much because math is hard—so is shooting three-pointers or making risotto—but because education makes it hard. Boring curriculum. Constant testing. Constant arguments over pedagogy. . .The guilt of being paid to shovel this anachronistic heap of emaciated and disconnected mathematics around finally caught up with me.

We often say that teachers have the hardest jobs, but that doesn't necessarily mean we should glorify those jobs. Some of the rules that teachers must follow are truly atrocious. Consider the observations of a professor in New York in 2015:

If, say, you are a teacher of 11th-grade English in Buffalo, you get, every 10 weeks, a thick three-ring binder with instructions on what you are to do in every class. The copy I have of one of these runs 587 pages. The volume is excruciatingly boring to read. (I cheated: I skimmed most of the pages.) I cannot imagine what it is like to be a creative and imaginative teacher hamstrung by it. Worse: I cannot imagine what it must be like to be a student in classes that now have to be taught by teachers forced to deliver this drivel or be fired.

For kids who are struggling day after day in school, the important distinction isn't about public versus private schools, urban versus suburban schools, or one curriculum versus another. I believe that the main culprit is control. In a conventional school, everyone is subject to heavy doses of arbitrary control: the teachers, the students, and even the parents (as evidenced by the arguments over homework and grades that disrupt countless households). The novelist Nicholson Baker neatly summarized the situation in his account of substitute teaching at high schools in Maine in 2014:

> Every day something like 16 million high-school students get up at the crack of dawn, slurp some oat clusters while barely conscious, hop on a bus, bounce around the county, show up and sit in a chair, zoned out, waiting for the first bell. If they're late, they are written up. Even if they don't do much academic work, they are physically present. Their attendance is a valuable commodity, because if students don't attend, teachers and guidance counselors and principals and textbook makers and designers of educational software have no jobs. A huge lucrative industry is built around them, and the students get nothing out of it but a G.P.A. They deserve not to have their time wasted. And it is wasted, as everyone knows. Teachers spend half their time shouting themselves hoarse, and young adults are infantilized. Their lives are absurdly regimented. Every minute is accounted for. They sit in one hot room after another and wait for each class to end. Time thickens. It becomes like saltwater taffy—it becomes viscous and sticky, and it stretches out and it folds back on itself through endless repetition. Tuesday is just like Wednesday, except the schedule is shuffled. Day after day of work sheets. By the time they graduate, they've done 13 years of work sheets.

While backpacking in New Zealand, I learned that high school students get to choose all of their classes in the final year (i.e., every class is an elective). In their second-to-last year, they get to choose every class except English. The year before that, every class except English, Math, and Science—and so on. Wonderful! As teenagers approach adulthood, the New Zealand education system gives them progressively more freedom. This makes sense, and it's a good move. It would be even better if students could enjoy the option of not attending any classes, but that would disrupt the control and childcare mandate of schooling. Sorry Kiwis; you're still conventional.

One thing that didn't make it onto my list of conventionality is size, which does matter: the smaller the school, the better. This is why the Small Schools Initiative had its heart in the right place when it proposed to keep schools under 200 total students and class sizes below 15 students. Yet despite having more than a billion dollars pumped into it, the Small Schools Initiative died a quiet death, as most public reform movements do.

The modern micro-school movement proposes to keep schools even smaller, to perhaps just a few dozen students *total*, with a focus on part-time attendance and using homeschooling laws to let families build highly flexible, personalized schedules. Bravo, micro-schools!

The smaller and more flexible a school becomes, the more likely that an individual student will feel a sense of belonging. But it all depends on how adults use their power. In that small, caring, and creative school where Grace Llewellyn worked, she noticed "an uglier flip side of [all] that individual attention: we teachers seemed to see or otherwise find out nearly everything about students' lives, and then hound students endlessly about things that were none of our business—missing homework assignments, social conflicts, messy notebooks. Even when we were not inclined to pry or push, students had little privacy, no way to escape our eyes." Control comes in all sizes.

In all likelihood, your local schools are big and conventional. And to be fair, these schools *do* work for some kids. My five younger siblings and I all grew up in conventional schools, a mix of public and private. We all got decent grades, received high school diplomas, went to college, found various forms of gainful employment, and stayed out of jail. Did conventional school work for us? At first glance, yes. But it's also hard to separate cause from effect. Did we turn out okay because of school or in spite of school? Who can we thank for turning out fine: our teachers, schools, parents, genes, or communities? All I can say for myself is that school probably didn't screw me up permanently.

Young people who thrive in conventional school, in my experience, tend to be among the following:

- Kids for whom school inflicts only minor amounts of stress and anxiety
- Kids who genuinely want to learn a little bit about every academic subject in a formal classroom environment
- Kids who derive meaning from the extracurriculars typically found at big schools like sports, drama, band, robotics, or mock trial[4]
- Kids who aren't labeled as having learning disabilities, such as ADHD
- Kids who build long-lasting friendships in school

---

4 If your kid loves one or more of these activities, don't write off alternative education just yet; in many U.S. states, homeschoolers are legally entitled to participate in public school extracurriculars.

- Kids who are seldom bullied or harassed
- Kids who are naturally conformist
- Kids with a history of unconventional education who voluntarily elect to return to school

I did fine in school, yet I only identify with less than half the points on that list. How about you? How about your kids?

Engagement, Boredom, and Stress

What does it mean for school to not work for a kid? There are many ways to answer this question, but let's begin with the idea of engagement. Here's how the polling organization Gallup defines it:

> Engaged students are excited about what's happening at their school and about what they're learning. They contribute to the learning environment and are psychologically committed to their school. Engaged students feel safe at school, have strong relationships with teachers and other students, feel recognized on a regular basis, and are learning important things that connect them to a positive future.

Gallup's 2016 poll of 900,000 North American public and private schoolers reported that student engagement fell from 74% to 32% between fifth grade and eleventh grade. Over that same period, the percentage of "actively disengaged" students rose from 8% to 34%. (The final 35% of eleventh graders were merely "not engaged.")

Lest anyone believe that it's okay for one-third of a school's eleventh graders to be "actively disengaged," consider how similarly labeled adults act in the workplace (also according to Gallup):

Actively disengaged employees are more or less out to damage their company. They monopolize managers' time; have more on-the-job accidents; account for more quality defects; contribute to 'shrinkage' or theft; are sicker; miss more days; and quit at a higher rate than engaged employees do. Whatever the engaged do—such as solving problems, innovating, and creating new customers—the actively disengaged try to undo.

What about boredom? Everyone feels bored at some point, so is it really a problem if students feel bored, or is it just an inescapable part of life? That's a valid question, and it's one that a group of researchers explored in a 2013 article published in the journal of *Motivation and Emotion*. The researchers identified five types of boredom, some of which were harmless (such as the zoned-out "indifferent boredom"), some positive (like the curiosity-kindling "searching boredom"), and one of which was downright dangerous: "apathetic boredom," which the authors describe as "an especially unpleasant form that resembles learned helplessness or depression." Unsurprisingly, this was the type of boredom that prevailed among the high schoolers sampled.

Many parents automatically ascribe superior status to private schools over public schools, but as the National Association of Independent Schools reported in 2016, 83% of private school students are sometimes or often bored, compared to 86% of public-school students—and their complaints were essentially the same as those of public schoolers. So, from the point of view of boredom, public and private schools are more or less equal. In 2015 a 17-year-old named Nick Bain illustrated this reality when he decided to write down exactly what he was doing every 15 minutes at his fancy, $30,000 per year school in Denver, Colorado. In the seven-hour school day, he calculated, there were only "2 1/2 to three hours that you actually really do need to be in class" to get relevant instruction from the teachers. "It occurred to me," Bain graciously summarized, "that maybe the way school is now is not the perfect way."

Then there's the stress. A 2014 report from the American Psychological Association (APA) revealed that the average teenager is more stressed than the average adult, and 83% of teenagers blame school for their stress. Most revealing was the fact that "extreme stress" levels doubled during the school year and then returned to normal in the summer.

Dig into that same APA report, and you'll see that 71% of adults are stressed about money, 69% are stressed about work, and 59% are stressed about the economy. So, isn't stress just a part of life? Might it even be a good thing to prepare young people for the many stresses of life?

Sometimes, yes; but like boredom, it's helpful to distinguish between the varieties. According to the National Scientific Council on the Developing Child, there are three broad categories of childhood stress:

- Positive stress is "a normal and essential part of healthy development, characterized by brief increases in heart rate and mild elevations in hormone levels." Imagine rock climbing for the first time, preparing for a big talk, or doing anything else that's both exciting and scary.
- Tolerable stress "activates the body's alert systems to a greater degree as a result of more severe,

longer-lasting difficulties, such as the loss of a loved one, a natural disaster, or a frightening injury." If tolerable stress is short-term and supported by caring adults, a kid will recover without damage. For example, I was occasionally bullied in middle school; it was unpleasant but tolerable.

- Toxic stress is "strong, frequent, and/or prolonged adversity—such as physical or emotional abuse, chronic neglect, caregiver substance abuse or mental illness, exposure to violence, and/or the accumulated burdens of family economic hardship—without adequate adult support." Or as Ned Johnson and Bill Stixrud put it in *The Self-Driven Child*, toxic stress is when a "child perceives that he or she has little control over what happens. There seems to be no reprieve, no cavalry coming, no end in sight."

In a perfect world, all childhood stress would be positive. Alas, that is not our world, and it's not just underprivileged kids who get the worst of it. According to psychologist Madeline Levine, it is the "preteens and teens from affluent, well-educated families [who] experience among the highest rates of depression, substance abuse, anxiety disorders, somatic complaints, and unhappiness of any group of children in [the United States]."

Chronically stressed kids don't turn into high-performing adults when the "parts of the brain that are responsible for memory, reasoning, attention, judgment, and emotional control are dampened and eventually damaged," as Stixrud and Johnson point out in *The Self-Driven Child*, making them "far more likely to develop anxiety disorders, depression, and a host of other mental and physical problems." Positive stress is good. Too much stress, especially of the tolerable and toxic varieties, is clearly destructive.

Most adults don't actually want to lead highly stressful lives, and neither do young people. It's simply not a good goal. No one wants to be constantly bored, disengaged, anxious, or stressed—yet these are the demons that conventional school persistently breeds.

These are also, I believe, the best metrics with which to determine whether conventional school is working for your kid. Forget the grades, forget the teachers' reports, forget the awards and accolades. Focus on engagement, boredom, and stress. Does your kid seem highly engaged in their school? Are they seldom bored? Is the stress manageable? If so, fantastic! Perhaps that's where they belong, at least for now. If not, it's time to start exploring alternatives.

To these alternatives we now turn, starting with the most conventional and progressing toward the least conventional.

Progressive and Experiential Schools

Our journey begins with the classic progressive alternative schools that originated in Europe in the first half of the twentieth century: Montessori, Waldorf, and Reggio Emilia. In such schools, teachers create aesthetically pleasing and stimulating environments, students are given large degrees of choice and voice, and classes are small and of mixed ages. Because these models are generally well-known—they're the first thing most people associate with the phrase "alternative school"—I won't spend much time describing their methods and positive attributes.

Progressive alternative schools serve many children well, but two major facts hinder them: there are few options for older children, and, all things considered, they are still quite conventional.

If you're a parent of a young child in a large city, you'll likely enjoy a wide choice of progressive schools. Where I'm from in Northern California, for example, it's difficult to throw a stone and not hit a Montessori preschool.[5] Move into the elementary school years, and the options begin to dwindle. Come middle and high school, Reggio Emilia schools are gone and Montessori schools are rare. Waldorf high schools do exist, but their tuition rates trend toward the stratosphere. The result is that most kids who attend progressive schools when they're young tend to end up in conventional schools when they're older.

Despite their holistic and child-centered philosophies, many progressive schools still employ the tools of conventional schools. Peter Gray observes that the progressive vision rests upon a collaboration between the child and a "benevolent, extraordinarily competent teacher, who gently guides the child's energy and shapes the child's raw ideas in ways that serve the child's and society's long-term good." Note the verbs *guide* and *shape*, which can quickly become synonymous with *control*. Coercion often still exists in progressive schools; it just comes in the form of a white glove instead of a balled fist. This becomes more apparent for older students when they are expected to increasingly conform to a standard academic curriculum.

---

5 Fun fact: the term "Montessori" is not legally protected, which means anyone can start a "Montessori school." *Caveat emptor.*

If your kid doesn't fundamentally reject the coercive machinery of schooling and just needs a slightly more creative or emotionally sensitive environment, a progressive school might be a great choice.

Emerging from the middle- and high-school cliff where progressive schools tend to disappear come a smattering of private independent schools that combine academics with travel, service, outdoor adventure, and other hands-on experiences for teenagers. These are mostly based in the United States but accept students from all over the world. My favorite examples include the 13 members of the Semester Schools Network and alternative boarding schools like the Arthur Morgan School (which you'll learn more about in Chapter 3).

As with progressive schools, watch out for conventionality hiding behind the mask of "experiential learning" in some private schools. All of these schools have some form of compulsory academics, but the program's campus, community, and extracurriculars may tip the scales in favor of a positive experience. I've also known teenagers who hated conventional academics but loved their classes in experiential schools.

Finally, falling somewhere along the experiential-progressive spectrum are what I call the "somewhat self-directed techie alternatives." These schools cluster around urban hubs like San Francisco, Brooklyn, and Austin, and tend to cater to high-income families who work in the technology and innovation sectors. These are the Acton Academies, Fusion Academies, and Brightworks of the world. They're evolving so quickly that it makes little sense for me to discuss them individually. Like the progressive and experiential schools, they're all somewhat conventional, but their particular flavor might fit your kid, at least for a while.

Virtual and Hybrid Schools

Virtual schools (a.k.a. online schools) are on the rise in some states in the U.S., offering an affordable alternative for kids who just need to get away from the physical reality of school and enjoy the freedom to study at their own pace and in their own way. Some virtual schools are public and cost-free. Others are private and low-cost. Most follow a standard curriculum.

Some public-school districts are upping their game with "hybrid schooling" or "blended learning" which signifies an overlap between brick-and-mortar school and homeschooling. A mom from Santa Cruz, California, gushed to me about two public hybrid schools in her area—Ocean Alternative School and Alternative Family Education—that serve kids of all stripes: those who are highly academic, those more averse to academics, and those with special needs and learning disabilities. At these hybrid schools, students choose between a wide selection of in-person classes, online classes, extracurriculars, field trips, and social events. They can receive academic credit for self-directed learning at home, take community college classes, and drop into classes (such as Advanced Placement classes) at the local public school. Hybrid schools often require you to meet with an advisor each month, and that person will definitely push you in the direction of the state curriculum. Public school dollars come with attached strings, but the flexibility may be worth it.

Homeschooling

Growing up, I believed that homeschooling was a strange thing practiced only by families more religious, conservative, or kooky than my own. Why would anyone think or care about homeschooling?

How wrong I was. Now I see homeschooling for what it really is: a hard-won, highly inclusive, and incredibly powerful privilege that's worth celebrating and defending.

Homeschooling, when properly understood, is not an instructional method. It doesn't have to mean "doing school at home." Think of it instead as a Get Out of Jail Free card for young people who don't fit into public school and can't afford (or don't want) to attend private school. Regulations vary from place to place, but at its core, homeschooling laws give parents and young people *carte blanche* to design an educational path that fits them best.

Before we proceed, I'd like to share some basic facts about homeschooling and address some of the most common stereotypes that you may be harboring, as I did for so long. These facts all pertain to the United States, where homeschooling culture is the strongest.

Homeschooling has been legal everywhere in the United States since 1993. According to the National Center for Education Statistics (NCES), about 3% of school-aged kids are homeschooled in the U.S., which is about 2 million, total—and that number is generally believed to be low, because some states do not require families to report their children as homeschoolers.

Homeschooling is regulated on a state-by-state basis with roughly 20 states requiring some form of regular academic assessment. New York, Pennsylvania, and Washington state are the most restrictive. Yet even in homeschool-hostile New York, homeschooled kids choose among six different state-approved tests, which they only need to take every other year for grades 1–8 and every year for grades 9–12, and score above the thirty-third percentile.

On the other end of the regulation spectrum in California, where parents must only file a single piece of (online) paperwork each October—the "private school affidavit"—that declares their home to be a private school and subsequently fulfills their child's compulsory education requirement. Ta-da, you're done! California law requires parents to provide instruction in all the traditional academic subjects, but it also restricts the state's ability to verify this. So, California homeschooling families can do essentially whatever they want. If a state official showed up at your door, they would only be allowed to ask for attendance records, which you could whip up in roughly the same amount of time that it takes to brew a cup of coffee for your visitor.[6]

---

6 The origins of highly permissive homeschooling laws in the United States are fascinating. It all started when two Supreme Court rulings in the 1960s held that school-sponsored prayer and Bible readings violated the First Amendment, which deeply offended many Christians and conservatives, as did the recent entrance of sex education and evolution into public school curricula. This spurred the creation of thousands of Christian day schools that successfully resisted governmental oversight—such as the requirement to have state-certified teachers or to deliver any amount of traditional curriculum—in the name of religious freedom. The newly formed Homeschool Legal Defense Association waged a state-by-state campaign to ensure that homeschooling became legal and largely unregulated all over the US. These policies subsequently aided the efforts of the more left-leaning reformers and homeschooling families of the 1970s and onwards, instigating a rare alliance between conservatives and liberals (John Holt used the term "odd bedfellows" in 1979) that would seem impossible to pull off in today's political climate.

In a nutshell, homeschooling is free, legal, and mostly unregulated across the United States. That doesn't mean that it's automatically accessible to all, of course, because most children require supervision, and the cost of one parent staying home is too high for many families. (The growing number of drop-off programs and micro-schools for homeschoolers is changing this.) But the opportunity to homeschool is genuinely equal under the eyes of the law.

Demographically speaking, the stereotypical homeschooler is white, conservative, and Christian. But the sands are shifting. Here are a few statistics from the most recent NCES survey of homeschoolers, published in 2016:

- Race: 59% of homeschoolers identify as non-Hispanic whites, 8% as non-Hispanic blacks, 3% as Asian, and a whopping 26% as Hispanic—a massive jump from the 7% of Hispanics reported just four years prior. For comparison, the U.S. public school population has a somewhat smaller portion of white students (50%), twice as many black students (15.6%), and a similar portion of Hispanic students (24%).
- Language: Approximately 15% of homeschooled children live in a family where one or both parents do not speak English.
- Income: 21% of homeschoolers are considered poor. For comparison, 24% of public-school students attend "high-poverty" schools.
- Parent credentials: About 45% of homeschooling parents hold a bachelor's or master's degree, 25% have a vocational degree or some college, 16% have

only a high school diploma, and 15% have no diploma. (For comparison, in 2016, about 33% of adults in the U.S. held a bachelor's degree or higher.)

- Reason for homeschooling: The top three stated motivations for homeschooling include "concern about the school environment" (34%), "dissatisfaction with academic instruction at school" (17%), and a "desire to provide religious instruction" (16%). Just nine years earlier, the religious motivation held the top position at 37%.

Translation: While homeschoolers are still more likely to be white and have college-educated parents, they're also becoming less religious, and they're looking increasingly similar to the overall U.S. population.

What about the stereotype of the isolated or unsocialized homeschooler, or the homeschooler who merely does school-at-home in a highly controlled and parent-directed fashion? Professors Robert Kunzman and Milton Gaither reviewed more than 1,400 academic texts related to homeschooling in 2013 in order to shine a light on such assumptions. They concluded that homeschoolers do, in fact, "learn vital social skills that help them interact successfully in broader society." Social isolation does become an issue for older homeschoolers, which is why "homeschooling grows less common as children age, even among highly educated, more affluent families." And most homeschooling parents do end up giving their kids a significant voice in their educational destinies, seeing how "after a year or two of assiduous effort to mimic formal schooling at home, homeschooling mothers gradually move toward a less-structured, more eclectic approach."

Modern homeschooling is diverse, flexible, and simply not fringe anymore. It's an incredible privilege that we in North America and a handful of other countries enjoy. May it spread further across the world.

Defining Unconventionality

Thus far we've been exploring the somewhat-conventional alternatives: ones that are still driven by parents, teachers, and curriculum, and ones that don't rustle too many feathers. If you've found something here that works for your kid, wonderful. If not, hold on to your hat—because now we'll dive into the world of truly unconventional alternatives.

In my eyes, an unconventional school is one that discards as many artificial and unnecessary barriers to learning, growth, and interpersonal connection as possible. Such places tend to feature:

- No mandatory curriculum or standardized testing
- No grades or other written assessments (unless requested)
- Full age-mixing
- Significant decision-making power for young people
- High autonomy for adult staff
- High freedom for physical movement
- High personal privacy
- Open campus
- Flexible arrival and departure hours

What does this look like in practice? Imagine that you've been granted the right to spend a day at a small unconventional school. You're thinking about sending your kid here, but you want to check it out first.

With your visitor badge on, you wander around the halls for a half hour waiting for something to happen. But nothing happens, at least, not in the way that you were expecting. Young people of all ages are hanging out, playing games, interacting with screens, reading books, and chatting. You notice some adult staff around, but they're mostly doing their own thing. No one is barking orders at the kids, except when a group gets too boisterous and a staff member reminds them to tone it down or take it outside.

You discover a schedule posted on the wall with a few class titles that reassure you: writing, history, math. But those are far outweighed by offerings in the realm of music, dance, drama, field trips, and projects with code names you can't yet decipher.

You join a history class that only has four kids, albeit four highly engaged kids. When the kids need to go to the bathroom, they just go to the bathroom. The whole thing is more reminiscent of the small-group seminar you remember from college than any classroom from your K–12 days.

Back in the common area, the majority of young people are looking at screens: some by themselves, others with friends. A small group clusters around a set of desktop computers, immersed in the blocky world of Minecraft. In the quiet room, a few kids are reading. In the kitchen, a group is casually chatting. Three high-energy kids are running around outside despite the frigid weather.

You have a moment of panic. "This isn't how school is supposed to feel," you tell yourself. No one is nervously preparing for a test. No one is being lectured to or doing homework. No one is being questioned by an adult, aside from that conversation you passed in the kitchen, where a staff member was challenging three adolescents' beliefs about vegetarianism.

What's so unnerving about this place? You dwell on this question for a moment. Maybe it's the fact that these kids don't seem to be worrying about their futures. Maybe it's the fact that the whole place feels too open, relaxed, accepting, and free. Kids, open your eyes! Don't you know it's a cold, harsh world out there? You can't afford to be this relaxed! Get to work!

As the day ends, you notice that most kids just wander out the front door. A few parents pop in, give their kid a hug, and walk out together to the car. Some kids take the public bus, others get rides with friends. You wait for the final bell—a conditioned response from your own years in school—but it never comes. In fact, you haven't heard a single bell all day.

Sudbury, Agile Learning Centers, and Liberated Learners

Quiz question: Where have you just spent the day?

1. A Sudbury school
2. An Agile Learning Center
3. A Liberated Learners center

Never heard any of these names before? Don't worry; even if you guessed randomly, you're correct.

There are few places in our culture that truly empower young people to be in control of their choices, spaces where children face few requirements and can genuinely decline the invitations of adults. Sudbury schools, Agile Learning Centers, and Liberated Learners centers are such places. Here, kids get to choose what they do for essentially the whole day, even if that looks like "doing nothing." This is as unconventional as it gets.[7]

Sudbury schools are a type of democratic free school, and they've been around since the late 1960s when the original Sudbury Valley School opened its doors. Agile Learning Centers and Liberated Learners centers have emerged more recently. Each is a coalition of independently operated member organizations, and these organizations are almost always private and not-for-profit. Needless to say, virtually none qualify for public funding.[8]

These schools and centers are small—with a total enrollment between 10 and 150—and most serve the full age spectrum, 5 to 18, under the same roof. Liberated Learners centers typically enroll just middle- and high-school aged kids. While each takes a different approach, they all fundamentally offer the same things:

- A stable, welcoming, and supportive community for young people
- Unrestricted free play and age-mixing

---

7 For a detailed cross-comparison of these three popular models, find the article I wrote for The Alliance for Self-Directed Education in 2018: "Agile Learning Centers, Liberated Learners, and Sudbury Schools: What's the Difference?"

8 In the U.S., it is sometimes possible to use the funds provided by virtual charter schools to help pay for attendance at schools and centers like these. And outside of the U.S., some democratic free schools do receive public funding.

- No mandatory tests, labeling of students, or judgement of what's "okay" to learn
- No manipulation (whether subtle or overt) of young people by adults
- Meaningful relationships with adults based on natural authority, not arbitrary power
- Deep respect for the power of self-direction to drive the learning process
- Restorative justice instead of punitive justice (while maintaining non-negotiable rules against violence, assault, property destruction, law-breaking, etc.)[9]

Places like these diverge so radically from our conventional beliefs about children, work, and education, that it's normal to feel resistance in the beginning. It's difficult to move past the notion that kids must be working on something—anything—for most of the day. It takes a while to adapt to a space where kids are not being compelled to do things that adults deem productive: a space where "nothing" seems to be happening.

So much does happen at Sudbury schools, Agile Learning Centers, and Liberated Learners centers—it's just hard to measure and categorize. Jim Rietmulder, co-founder of the Sudbury-inspired Circle School in Pennsylvania, penned the best answer I've yet found to the question of what kids do at a school like his:

---

9 Schools that follow the classic Sudbury Valley School model employ a justice system that may be better labeled "retributive."

[They] may hang out with friends, build a fantasy world with wooden blocks, organize a math class, work at a community externship, do "nothing," play Capture the Flag outdoors, browse the web, build a virtual world in a cyber simulation, take a nap, earn money doing extra chores, obsess over social media and pop culture, write a blog post, attend Spanish classes, produce a video, run a committee meeting, organize a blues band, paint a mural, take apart a microwave oven, operate a business, teach a friend to apply makeup, learn chess, make and sell baked goods, create a school corporation, prepare to take college entry exams, advocate for legislation, give an election campaign speech, put on a play, organize a week-long backpacking expedition, build a Tesla coil, and so on from daily novelty to creative infinity.

To put it another way: kids at Sudbury schools, Agile Learning Centers, and Liberated Learners centers enjoy the maximum possible liberty to direct their lives and educations—all day, every day.

Such liberty has bounds. As Rietmulder puts it, Circle School students are constrained by "imagination and school laws, but not by curriculum or adult demands." Communities like these also recognize that they're members of a broader society: a society which would undoubtedly (and thankfully) shut down any school that encouraged 5-year-olds to play unsupervised with power tools, break local laws, or traumatize each other.

This liberty also exists within the financial constraints faced by small non-profit organizations. While in college I volunteered at a small Sudbury-model school that inhabited a cramped office space alongside a busy four-lane road. On rainy days, the school was noisy, crowded, and chaotic. The two full-time staff members were kind, generous, dedicated, and forever struggling to keep their ship afloat while paying themselves poverty wages. The school closely followed the model of the Sudbury Valley School, but it lacked the flagship school's resources (a stone mansion on 10 acres of picturesque New England countryside with an adjacent nature preserve) and high enrollment. The handful of teenage members felt isolated in a sea of younger children. Life at this school wasn't pretty at times, but I still witnessed kids thriving there. If you were a young person who needed genuine respect and autonomy in your life, this struggling little non-profit was still the best game in town.

While most of these schools and centers are technically tuition-charging private institutions, most charge far less than typical private schools, and many offer generous financial aid and work-trade opportunities. The founders of such places are often concerned about inclusion, accessibility, and building a world where everyone can pursue self-directed education. Many have forsaken lucrative opportunities (such as six-figure public-school contracts) to dedicate themselves to working in a purpose-driven field with near-zero prospects of government funding or support from charitable foundations. These places may not be financially accessible to all, but in my experience, they're as accessible as humanly possible.

Can highly unconventional schools and centers scale to serve larger populations? The typical answer is no—the smallness is part of the magic—but one model offers inspiration: Village Home in Portland, Oregon. Founded in

2002, Village Home is sort of like a community college for homeschoolers. Young people choose from a large selection of classes (over 200 at their main campus), none of which have grades or tests. In a select number of classes, there are student assignments that teachers give informal feedback on, but most classes do not require "output" by the student. The average class size is 10, and most students attend just five hours a week. There's no required curriculum, and the class schedule is largely inspired by student and parent requests. Each of their three campuses offers dedicated lounge areas for hang-out time for learners and their families.

Sudbury schools, Agile Learning Centers, and Liberated Learners centers—as well as democratic free schools and other unaffiliated organizations like Village Home—are wonderful places, and unfortunately, they remain rare. If you have one in your proverbial backyard, count your lucky stars, and then set up a visiting day.

Unschooling

What if you love the ideas that radical alternative schools espouse, but no such places exist in your area? Or perhaps one does exist, but you can't afford it?

What if you've had success with formal homeschooling—but now your kid is pushing back against the idea of you acting as teacher/principal/guidance counselor?

What if you feel a deep need to keep your young child close to home after seeing the harm that conventional school inflicted?

What if your kid, no matter their age, is simply allergic to all forms of imposed structure and obligation? What if they simply need maximum freedom and minimal restriction at this moment in their life?

Welcome, friends, to the end of the rainbow.

Unschooling combines the principles of unconventional schools with the freedom of homeschooling laws to create a powerfully flexible approach. Some people prefer to call it self-directed learning, child-led learning, or interest-led learning. In the eyes of the law, unschoolers are simply homeschoolers. But the two approaches can be worlds apart. Describing her unschooled upbringing, the filmmaker Astra Taylor wrote:

> We differed from homeschoolers in essential ways. We weren't replicating school at home. We had no textbooks, class times, deadlines, tests, or curricula. Were we fascinated by primates? By rocks? By baseball cards or balloon animals? If so, it was our duty to investigate. My parents eschewed coercion and counted on our curiosity, which they understood to be a most basic human capacity.

The line between parent-led homeschooling and self-directed unschooling is not always clear, and many families weave between the two worlds—that's the meaning of "eclectic homeschooling."

The writer and grown unschooler Idzie Desmarais muses on the different motives that may inform different families' homeschooling experiences:

> Was it their parents' intent. . .to allow them more freedom, more exploration, more meaningful relationships, more engagement? Or was the purpose to isolate them from the "wrong" influences, "wrong" ideas, "wrong" people?

More freedom and exploration is unschooling; more isolation and sheltering is (conventional) homeschooling.

Patrick Farenga, the publisher of John Holt's works, defines unschooling as "allowing your children as much freedom to explore the world around them in their own ways as you can comfortably bear." The words *comfortably bear* are vital, because they emphasize the importance of the parent-child relationship. If you give your kid more freedom than you can comfortably bear, then at some point you're likely to freak out, clamp down, and undo much of the progress you've made together. Unschooling is a journey on which parent and child embark together, sort of like a partnered dance where the roles of leader and follower are not always clear.

What is the role of an unschooling parent? Broadly speaking, it is to expand your definition of freedom, to bear progressively more discomfort, and to help your child explore the world without choosing their specific direction through the world. Or as unschooling mother Ana Martin puts it:

> My job is to approach them with humility and know that my ability to discern what they are to be or to do or to excel in is nothing compared to theirs. My job is to assist them in their discernment. To make experiences, work, play, resources, teachers, mentors, and collaborators available to them to help them as they construct themselves. To talk things through with them, but not talk it all to death. . . I direct nothing. Less of me. More of them.

From a learning perspective, nothing is off the table for unschoolers. They learn online, offline, through books, through work, and through play. Unschoolers may experiment with part-time or short-term school attendance, despite the seeming contradiction with their self-assigned label. Yet the contradiction disappears when you begin to realize that unschooling isn't anti-school or anti-structure; it's about applying the notion of consent to the realm of education.

In the dozen years I've worked in this arena, I've seen unschooled teenagers sign up for all manner of highly structured activities: community college classes, test-prep tutoring, language schools, music lessons, martial arts, and boot-camp-style retreats. Some choose to do virtual school, while others follow the Khan Academy curriculum to learn math and science. Yet in all these structured and school-like activities, these young people remain unschoolers because their participation is fully their own choice.[10]

For kids coming out of conventional school (or highly structured, parent-driven homeschooling), unschooling begins with an adjustment period called "deschooling." (This happens at self-directed schools and centers, too.) During the deschooling period, a parent should truly ask nothing of her child beyond remaining a respectful human being. An oft-repeated rule of thumb is to give her one month of no-strings-attached deschooling for every year that she was previously in conventional school. Let her sit in front of screens, play games, and otherwise veg out without any

---

10   Some unschooling families take the principles of unschooling and apply them to parenting as a whole. These are the "radical unschoolers" who believe that limiting bedtimes, eating habits, screen time, and many other things is damaging to the parent-child relationship. You can adopt the radical approach, or you can keep your education and parenting silos separate; I'm agnostic on the subject. For the purposes of this book, when we talk about unschooling, don't assume it's the radical variety.

meddling influence on your part. Deschooling is the work of adjusting to a new reality, one in which a young person now possesses an extremely high level of freedom and a correspondingly high level of responsibility.

At first glance, unschooling might appear easy to the point of neglect. (Don't want to be bothered with educating your kids? Just let them do whatever they want!) Yet unschooling is anything but easy. It requires a reevaluation of your role as parent, leading to plenty of moments of anxiety, second-guessing, and potential conflict. A drama analogy may help: if school is scripted acting, then unschooling is improv. Each is challenging in its own way.

Agile Learning Centers, Liberated Learners centers, democratic free schools, and Sudbury schools are closely aligned with unschooling, although such communities do offer a communal experience that home-based unschooling does not easily reproduce. Taking part in the democratic processes of a Sudbury school, for example, teaches important lessons about civics and navigating institutions beyond the family. So it's not right to say that unschooling and radical alternative schools are the same thing, but both demand that parents make the same inner journey of relinquishing a sense of control.

Some families prefer the label "worldschooling," which typically indicates a traveling lifestyle. Worldschooling families may travel full-time in an RV, live abroad as expats, migrate between summer and winter home-bases, or do long-distance bike trips with their kids quite literally in tow. "The world is our classroom," goes the refrain. Some worldschoolers are closer to eclectic homeschoolers than unschoolers; after their kids finish the pick-up soccer game in Honduras, they do some parent-assigned math homework.

The reality is that most families don't stick with one label forever, because it makes sense to migrate between different styles of homeschooling and levels of imposed structure as kids grow and change. The trend is for families to go from formal homeschooling towards unschooling, but that's not a rule. Sometimes an unschooled kid desperately craves a large peer group, so he decides to join an alternative school for a few years. Sometimes the whole family desires novelty and adventure over everything else, so they hit the road for a few months and live the worldschooling lifestyle. Some teenage unschoolers I've known genuinely want to experience conventional high school, so they give it a shot for a semester or two. If it works for them, wonderful! If not, they know they can always leave and unschool again.

I'll say it one more time: it is not easy to unschool. As a parent, you must remain incredibly open and non-dogmatic. As soon as you develop a clear vision of how unschooling will turn out for your kid—he'll become a prolific writer; she'll become a skilled outdoorswoman; they'll go to graduate school—you're setting yourself up for failure.

The writer Ben Hewitt unschooled his son Fin from birth, yet Fin's interests eventually led him back to school. A dogmatic unschooling parent might attempt to dissuade his child from going to school, but Hewitt and his wife chose to welcome this turn of fate:

> I've watched as Fin's interest in music has become a driving force in his life, leading him to seek out an apprenticeship with a master guitar builder and, ultimately, to

part-time enrollment in a public school with a unique student-led program that has them composing songs, booking gigs, touring, and recording. Fin loves the social opportunities school provides, along with the chance to immerse himself even more completely in music. And while it was initially difficult for [my wife] Penny and me to see him walk through those doors, there is no denying that the life of my unschooled son is richer for the public-education system. Many times I have had to remind myself that just as I encourage others to challenge their assumptions regarding education, so too is it healthy to challenge my own.

Unschooling is just one answer to the question of "how do I help my struggling kid?" Other times, alternative school may be the answer. Other times still, formal homeschooling, virtual school, or community college may be the answer. And sometimes, even conventional school is the answer. Your kid is not the same person year after year, nor is she a mere vessel through which you might explore trendy educational ideas. She is her own person with evolving needs and capacities. Unschooling, properly understood, is about carefully observing your child, seeing what engages her, and employing your knowledge to reduce her needless suffering as she navigates this world.

I encourage you to fly no flag. Don't join the unschoolers and never look back. Instead, pledge allegiance only to the young person in your charge. Familiarize yourself with the full spectrum of options. Whenever you feel like you've found the answer to your kid's educational needs, add the words: for now.

Making the Leap

Kim Chin-Gibbons—the young woman in Western Massachusetts who suffered from a sleep disorder, barely passed the eighth grade, and saw her love for music and reading rapidly declining—quit school two weeks into her freshman year. She and her parents began searching for local alternatives and soon discovered North Star, a self-directed learning center for teenagers (and the model on which the Liberated Learners centers are based).

Kim joined the North Star community and immediately felt a difference. "Everyone accepted me and my quirky illnesses," she said. She began playing guitar again and joined multiple bands with other North Star teens, who also inspired her to explore photography. She secured an internship with a local photographer, built up her skills, and started tutoring other teens in both photography and guitar.

Now 17, Kim is in her fourth year at North Star. She was hired to do social media for a local artist-owned ensemble theatre group, where she spent the last year as an unpaid marketing intern. Kim has many friends, low stress, and her health is under control—and she's thinking about which colleges she'll apply to.

Tom Ochwat—the bored and stressed high schooler who had to be hospitalized for clinical depression and anxiety—returned to his junior year at conventional school optimistic about his prospects, but he knew within a month that it wouldn't work.

He and his parents scanned the Chicago suburbs and found Tallgrass, a small democratic free school based on the Sudbury model; a week later, Tom was enrolled, and he happily spent the rest of his junior and senior year there. He graduated from this school at the normal age, and he's now enrolled at DePaul university in Chicago, which he's "super excited about"—something Tom would never have said about the conventional schools of his past.

Gavin Lake, the one who could always "get by" in school—at least until he started arguing with his parents every night about homework and wishing he could just make films— told his mom at the beginning of sophomore year that he didn't want to go to school anymore. She obliged, and they began homeschooling, which quickly transformed into unschooling. For the next 18 months, Gavin dedicated his life almost exclusively to film; he wrote screenplays, directed movies with his friends, and taught film to kids at a summer camp.

In the fall of (what would have been) his senior year of high school, Gavin wasn't in school, nor was he in his hometown of Omaha, Nebraska—because he was in Seattle, beginning his first year at the Seattle Film Institute.

Vanessa Reyes, the girl from Charlotte who desperately hated school, ended up joining ALC Mosaic, an Agile Learning Center that her mom discovered.

Following a quick adjustment period, Vanessa thrived. "After a few weeks I didn't have all my anxiety symptoms anymore," she told me. "I trusted the adults way more. I was less prone to the incredibly aggressive behavior I had at my old school. I slowly began to have interests again because I finally had time for them, like ukulele, guitar, learning Japanese language, Japanese cooking, and just regular cooking." She enjoyed the relaxing, non-competitive, and warm community of ALC Mosaic for four years.

Now, at age 12, Vanessa is planning to go back to conventional school. Why? "I need a larger group of kids that are my age," she said, and she also wants to have "a normal middle school experience." Vanessa is even excited for the "forced-upon structure" of school again.

"Basically, I'm going to try to balance what people want me to do and what I want for myself. After four years at ALC Mosaic, I know I can go back to traditional school and thrive there. It's my choice, and I'll probably feel less anxiety, balance my life better, and know that how people judge me doesn't really matter."

For some kids, conventional school just isn't a good fit. It fuels anxiety and depression. It leaves them bored, disengaged, or mired in stress. It turns every assignment, test, and grade into trench warfare, pitting your kid against the system and you against your kid. The collateral damage can take years (or decades) to repair.

The Kims, Toms, Gavins, and Vanessas of the world don't need more encouragement to try harder in school. They don't need a different classroom. They need to escape conventional school, maybe just for a little while, or maybe forever.

The escape hatch will look different depending on where you live, what you can afford, and what your kid's needs are today. If Kim didn't live near North Star, perhaps she would have found a virtual public school or progressive school that felt like a good fit. Perhaps she would have unschooled. The important part is that she and her parents started searching for alternatives instead of trying to make the same old thing work.

Notes

For practical resources related to this chapter—and every other chapter in the book—please visit the book's dedicated webpage: https://blakeboles.com/y/

A Few Brief Stories

I obtained Kim's, Tom's, Gavin's, and Vanessa's stories via personal communication in 2018 (which is the timeframe in which the stories are set) and confirmed their details in early 2020. By request, Vanessa Reyes and Olivia Reyes are pseudonyms.

Defining Conventionality

On the freedom of adolescents compared to that of prison inmates or enlisted military personnel, see *The Case Against Adolescence* by Robert Epstein (2007).

Grace Llewellyn's quote about schools controlling students' lives is from *The Teenage Liberation Handbook* (1991), as is the Thoreau quote (which is originally from On Civil Disobedience).

The pediatric occupational therapist's quote is from "A therapist goes to middle school and tries to sit still and focus. She can't. Neither can the kids." by Valerie Strauss (December 3, 2014). https://www.washingtonpost.com/news/answer-sheet/wp/2014/12/03/a-therapist-goes-to-middle-school-and-tries-to-sit-still-and-focus-she-cant-neither-can-the-kids/

The math teacher quote is from "Why I quit teaching math" by Sunil Singh (October 9, 2017). https://beta.theglobeandmail.com/life/facts-and-arguments/i-love-math-but-quit-teaching-it-because-i-was-forced-to-make-it-dull-andbanal/article36526126/

The quote from the NY state professor is from "Dumbing Down the Kids" by Bruce Jackson (July 14, 2015). http://www.dailypublic.com/articles/07142015/dumbing-down-kids

The Nicholson Baker quote is from his article "Fortress of Tedium: What I Learned as a Substitute Teacher." (September 7, 2016). https://www.nytimes.com/2016/09/11/magazine/fortress-of-tedium-what-i-learned-as-a-substitute-teacher.html

On the life and death of the small schools movement, see "Small Schools: The Edu-Reform Failure That Wasn't" by Jack Schneider (February 9, 2016). https://www.edweek.org/ew/articles/2016/02/10/small-schools-the-edu-reform-failure-that-wasnt.html

On micro-schools, see "Are Microschools the Next Big Thing?" by Tyler Koteskey (March, 2018). https://reason.com/archives/2018/01/27/are-microschools-the-next-bi

Grace Llewellyn's quote about the flip side of individual attention is from *The Teenage Liberation Handbook* (1991).

On kids who appear to fit well into conventional school, see Denise Pope's book *Doing School* (2001). Pope follows students who succeed by conventional measures but do so at the expense of things like mental health and becoming passionate about anything.

Engagement, Boredom, and Stress

Gallup's definition of student engagement is from "School Engagement Is More Than Just Talk" by Tim Hodges (October 25, 2018). https://www.gallup.com/education/244022/school-engagement-talk.aspx

Gallup's definition of disengaged employees is from "Gallup's Employee Engagement Science" (undated, accessed November 26, 2019). https://q12.gallup.com/help/en-us/about

The 2016 Gallup poll of 900,000 North American public and private schoolers is from "Student Enthusiasm Falls as High School Graduation Nears" by Valerie J. Calderon and Daniela Yu (June 1, 2017). https://news.gallup.com/opinion/gallup/211631/student-enthusiasm-falls-high-school-graduation-nears.aspx

In his 2019 book, *More Joy More Genius*, educator Don Berg gathered Gallup student poll data from 2011–2016 and found that the number of engaged students has been steadily declining, while actively disengaged students have been steadily rising.

The National Association of Independent Schools 2016 report can be found at: https://www.fcis.org/uploaded/Data_Reports/2016-HSSSE_Final_1.pdf

On the five types of boredom, see "Boredom research has now become more interesting" by ScienceDaily (November 18, 2013). https://www.sciencedaily.com/releases/2013/11/131118103935.htm

Nick Bain's story: "To Learn More, This High-Schooler Left The Classroom" by Jenny Brundin (August 19, 2015). https://www.npr.org/sections/ed/2015/08/19/432582341/to-learn-more-this-high-schooler-left-the-classroom

I estimated the cost of Nick Bain's private school tuition to be $30,000 based on Colorado Academy's webpage, "Affordability: Tuition & Financial Aid" (undated, accessed November 28, 2019). https://www.coloradoacademy.org/page/admission/affordability-tuition--financial-aid

The 2014 report from the American Psychological Association about teenage stress is here: https://www.apa.org/news/press/releases/stress/2013/stress-report.pdf

The three types of stress are outlined on the webpage "Toxic Stress" by the Center on the Developing Child at Harvard University (undated, access

November 28, 2019). https://developingchild.harvard.edu/science/key-concepts/toxic-stress/

Madeline Levine's quote appeared in *Excellent Sheep* by William Deresiewicz (2014).

Progressive and Experiential Schools

Peter Gray's quote is from "Differences Between Self-Directed and Progressive Education" (June 27, 2017). https://www.psychologytoday.com/us/blog/freedom-learn/201706/differences-between-self-directed-and-progressive-education

Semester Schools Network: https://www.semesterschools.net/

A great place to look for experiential schools is the Davidson Institute's online resource database, specifically the "Educational Options: Alternative" category: http://www.davidsongifted.org/search-database

Virtual Schools

For more on hybrid schooling, see "Is Hybrid Homeschooling The Wave Of The Future?" by Mike McShane (May 21, 2018). https://www.forbes.com/sites/mikemcshane/2018/05/21/is-hybrid-homeschooling-the-wave-of-the-future/

On blended learning and cybercharters, see "Full-Time Virtual and Blended Schools: the 2018 NEPC Update" by Milton Gaither (February 8, 2019). http://icher.org/blog/?p=4134

Homeschooling

For general facts and figures about homeschooling in the United States, see "Homeschooling: Requirements, Research, and Who Does It" by Arianna Prothero (January 10, 2018). https://www.edweek.org/ew/issues/home-schooling/index.html. See also "The State of Homeschooling in America" by Elena Silva (September 21, 2018). https://psmag.com/education/the-state-of-home schooling-in-america

On the estimated numbers of homeschoolers being low, see "State Homeschool Policies: A patchwork of provisions" by Micah Ann Wixom (July 2015). http://www.ecs.org/clearinghouse/01/20/42/12042.pdf

New York state homeschooling regulations: http://www.nyhen.org/regs.htm

California homeschooling regulations: https://www.hsc.org/legal-101

On the origins of highly permissive homeschooling laws in the United States, see *Homeschooling: The History and Philosophy of a Controversial Practice* (2019) by James G. Dwyer and Shawn Francis Peters.

The race, language, and income statistics come from "Data Snapshot: Who Are the Nation's Homeschoolers?" by Sean Cavanagh (November 20, 2017) https://marketbrief.edweek.org/marketplace-k-12/data-snapshot-nations-homeschoolers/ as well as "NCES Homeschooling Data: First Look from 2016" by Robert Lyon (September 27, 2017). https://icher.org/blog/?p=3906 Note how the income comparison is flawed because the NCES uses the standard poverty line threshold, whereas federal data classifies "high-poverty" schools as those where more than 75% of students qualify for free or reduced-price lunches.

The recent jump in Hispanic homeschoolers is not yet well-understood and may be a statistical anomaly. The 2003 NCES survey, for example, found that black homeschoolers had dramatically jumped from their historic 4% representation to 9.4%. Then in 2007 the number sank back to 4%. It's also possible that more Hispanic families are homeschooling in order to raise bilingual kids or escape impoverished school districts. See "NCES Homeschooling Data: First Look from 2016" by Robert Lyon (September 27, 2017). https://icher.org/blog/?p=3906

More possible explanations for the recent jump in Hispanic homeschoolers are shared in "The New Face of U.S. Homeschooling is Hispanic" by Olivia Miltner (March 22, 2018). https://www.ozy.com/fast-forward/the-new-face-of-us-homeschooling-is-hispanic/85278

Parents' educational credentials are from the U.S. Census. See "Highest Educational Levels Reached by Adults in the U.S. Since 1940" (March 30, 2017). https://www.census.gov/newsroom/press-releases/2017/cb17-51.html

For Kunzman and Gaither's wonderfully detailed 2013 article, see "Homeschooling: A Comprehensive Survey of the Research" in *Other Education: The Journal of Educational Alternatives* (2013). Kunzman and Gaither are careful to highlight that most of the data is self-reported. https://othereducation.org/index.php/OE/article/view/10

Sudbury, Agile Learning Centers, and Liberated Learners

This section was adapted from my article "Agile Learning Centers, Liberated Learners, and Sudbury Schools: What's the Difference?" (December 6, 2018). https://www.self-directed.org/tp/three-popular-models/

Jim Rietmulder's quote is from *When Kids Rule the School* (2019).

Unschooling

Astra Taylor's quote is from her essay, "Unschooling" (2012). https://nplusonemag.com/issue-13/essays/unschooling/

Idzie Desmarais' quote is from "Homeschooling the Right Way: More of the World, Not Less" (August 7, 2018). http://yes-i-can-write.blogspot.

com/2018/08/homeschooling-right-way-more-of-world.html

Patrick Farenga's quote is from "The Foundations of Unschooling" (undated, accessed November 29, 2019). https://www.johnholtgws.com/the-foundations-of-unschooling. The quote is derived from a similar definition of unschooling made by John Holt.

Ana Martin's quote was published on her Facebook page, The Libertarian Homeschooler (October 25, 2013): https://www.facebook.com/TheLibertarian Homeschooler/posts/10151934239514424

I'm indebted to Ethan Mitchell for the notion of unschooling as consensual education, and I'm indebted to Kevin Currie-Knight for the improv analogy.

For a good overview of modern worldschooling, see: "Some Said They'd Flee Trump's America. These People Actually Did." by Ronda Kaysen (April 14, 2018) https://www.nytimes.com/2018/04/14/style/moving-to-canada-jk-traveling-until-2020.html (Ignore the clickbait title.)

Ben Hewitt's quote is from "The Case for Letting Kids Be Kids" (September 1, 2018). https://www.outsideonline.com/2339656/case-letting-kids-be-kids

2: THEY STILL GO TO COLLEGE AND GET GOOD JOBS

"But Does it Work?"

Every parent wants their kids to be able to go to college, find decent jobs, and live financially independent lives—which is why it can be incredibly scary to let them take a path that does not result in a traditional high school diploma.

Maybe you're not concerned about this. Maybe you're confident that your kid will turn out fine. But if your spouse, family members, or close friends don't share this confidence, taking an alternative path will be hard. You want these people on your team, and your dogged belief alone won't convince them. You'll need some solid arguments to prove that you're not ruining your kid's chances at a "normal life."

In this chapter I'll share what I've informally observed in my dozen years of working with teenage self-directed learners and witnessing them transitioning into adulthood. I'll also share the best research that we currently have about the outcomes of homeschooling, unschooling, and radical alternative schooling. Some of this research is strong; some is not. In general, we in the alternative education world are pretty bad about gathering data and making effective claims about the efficacy of these paths. I won't claim that all homeschoolers turn out fine because some of them get into Ivy League colleges, which is what some people concluded after David and Micki Colfax sent all their homeschooled kids to Harvard and then published their 1987 book, *Homeschooling for Excellence*.

In both the research and anecdotes, the bottom line is clear: the kids turn out alright. Alternative paths, including the most radical ones, consistently lead young people to college, career, and other forms of independent adulthood. The path is seldom straight, and each child's timeline will undoubtedly be different, but they all get where they need to go.

How They Do in College

The question that many parents first ask when considering homeschooling, unschooling, or attending a radically alternative school is "Will this adequately prepare my kid for the demands of a four-year college? If my child chooses to attend college, can I feel confident that she'll succeed despite her academically non-traditional upbringing?"

Let's start with homeschooling, where we have a few excellent pieces of research. Keep in mind that the term "homeschooling" indicates the full diversity of homeschoolers, including conventional school-at-home families, eclectic homeschoolers, unschoolers, and those who participate in virtual or hybrid programs.

In a 2016 study published in the journal *Educational Measurement: Issues and Practices*, researchers from the University of Minnesota compared 732 U.S. homeschoolers to a similar group of high school students. They found that the homeschoolers showed no difference in their freshman GPA, nor their retention rate (i.e., the likelihood of dropping out of college), compared to mainstream high schoolers. This is good news, especially considering that the researchers carefully matched the homeschoolers to high school students with comparable socioeconomic status and academic achievement levels.

Kunzman and Gaither's 2013 review of the scholarly homeschooling literature reached a similar conclusion. Most studies found "little to no difference on a wide range of variables between previously homeschooled and previously institutionally schooled students" in college performance, including retention rate, graduation rate, and emotional and social success. Homeschoolers did seem to hold more campus leadership positions than their conventionally schooled peers, and they struggled more with writing research papers in their first year—but soon caught up. Regarding acceptance rates, Kunzman and Gaither found that homeschoolers were neither favored nor discriminated against by college admissions boards. Their acceptance rates were approximately the same, even considering that many colleges "do not go out of their way to provide special services or admissions procedures for homeschoolers."

So, there you go. That's the best data we currently have about how homeschoolers do in college. It seems that homeschooling doesn't really make a difference in either direction.

Now, what about unschoolers specifically? Here the data is thinner. The most widely cited paper is a 2015 survey conducted by Peter Gray and Gina Riley that investigated the lives of 75 grown unschoolers. Gray and Riley discovered that 44% of the respondents had completed (or were in the process of completing) a bachelor's degree. This compares favorably to the percentage of U.S. adults who held bachelor's degrees in the same year, approximately 32%.

This is good news for unschooling, but we also need to take this finding with a grain of salt, because it represents a self-selected, volunteer group of unschoolers. It's possible that Gray and Riley received a disproportionate number of responses from those with positive unschooling experiences, rather than those whose unschooling "failed" in one way or another. The sample size was small, and they also did not collect information on family income, parental levels of education, or other potentially significant background variables. So this survey doesn't prove that unschoolers *will* do fine in college; it simply shows that *some* unschoolers have done fine in college. (As Gray himself observed, "this study, by itself, cannot be a basis for strong claims about the experiences and feelings of the whole population of unschoolers.")

That's pretty much it for unschooling research. What about the radical alternative schools and learning centers? Back in 1986, Peter Gray conducted a survey of Sudbury Valley School graduates that was very similar to his and Gina Riley's later survey of unschoolers, and it revealed that 45% of the school's alumni had received (or were in the process of receiving) a bachelor's degree. The school itself conducted another survey five years later, finding that 39% of its 188 graduates had received college degrees.

Ken Danford, executive director of North Star (the flagship member of the Liberated Learners network), conducted a similar survey in 2016. Of North Star's 267 alumni, at least 38% had attended 4-year college, which is a number very similar to the conventional attendance rate in Massachusetts, where North Star is located.

These surveys are good news for Sudbury schools, Liberated Learners centers, and similarly radical organizations—especially considering they surveyed all alumni, not just a self-selected group of volunteers.

A 2015 study conducted by The Circle School, a Sudbury-inspired democratic free school in Pennsylvania, achieved a greater level of nuance. The school's research team first demonstrated that the income profile of their students matched the income profile of the school's local area. Then they showed that their graduates were more likely to attend college (by roughly 10%) than kids from financially similar families nationwide. While their sample size was small—the school had only 78 total graduates in 2015—The Circle School did manage to show that their graduates' success was not completely the result of being financially advantaged.

Looking at the evidence as a whole, the radically alternative routes seem unlikely to alter a kid's college prospects. Unschoolers and radical alternative school graduates in North America attend a full range of institutions—including Ivy League schools—and they graduate at the same rate as their peers. Yet we must acknowledge that the research is thin, and part of these kids' success may be due to the fact that they come from "a special group of people to begin with who were destined to do well no matter what sort of education they had," as Gray mused in his 1983 paper. We simply won't know until better research is done.[11]

---

11 It's very challenging to do better research in this regard. As education professor Kevin Currie-Knight told me: "The problem is that any

In Chapter 4, we'll dive more deeply into the question of who should go to college. For now, rest assured that each of the alternatives described in this book can and do lead young people to successfully complete four-year degrees. Not only do these kids get where they need to go, but they almost certainly arrive there having wasted less time, experienced less stress, explored their interests more fully, and gained more self-awareness about the questions of "why college?" and "why now?" than they would have on the conventional path.

How They Get into College

How exactly do unconventional learners get into college? Don't they need an accredited high school diploma and a transcript showing X years of English, math, foreign language, etc.? The challenge seems overwhelming at the outset, but the near-universal story that North American homeschoolers, unschoolers, and alternative school students have told me over the years is this: *It's really not that hard.* They figure out what colleges want to see, fill in the gaps, and move forward.[12]

Below I detail the college admission process for

---

non-randomized study will be vulnerable to selection bias. Randomized research can't be done on unschoolers, almost by definition, as unschooling involves choice over educational trajectory. An unschooler forced to unschool for the purposes of a randomized trial is no longer an unschooler."

12   The advice in this chapter is North American-centric; college admissions are trickier for homeschoolers and alternative school students in other countries. In Europe and the U.K., for example, universities won't consider an unaccredited diploma; some sort of state-certified standardized tests are simply non-negotiable. Sometimes there are creative ways to take these exams without enrolling in conventional school; other times there aren't.

non-traditional students, which hasn't changed much since I published my first book dedicated to this topic, *College Without High School*, in 2009. Your specific process will always depend on the guidelines of the specific institutions to which you're applying, but in general, there are two broad routes to take: applying as a normal first-year student or as a transfer student.

For conventional students, the route for first-year student admissions looks like this:

- Take high school classes, get decent grades, graduate high school with an accredited diploma.
- Take the SAT or ACT, perhaps supplemented with AP tests and SAT Subject Tests.
- Apply to colleges as a normal first-year student.

The transfer admission process looks like this:

- Graduate high school, with or without decent grades
- Complete 1-2 years of community college classes at your own pace, getting decent grades.
- Apply to colleges as a normal transfer student.

The unconventional route does add a few steps, but it's not radically different. For those applying as first-year students, it looks like this:

- Engage in a variety of activities in your high school years, including some standard academics.
- Take the SAT or ACT, perhaps supplemented with AP tests and SAT Subject Tests.
- Take a handful of community college or dual

enrollment courses to prove that you can handle college-level academics.

- Create an unaccredited high school diploma (or get one from your alternative school) that presents your various learning experiences as "courses" with narrative descriptions.[13]
- Apply to college as a standard first-year student.

The unconventional route to becoming a transfer student is even easier:

- At age 18 (or earlier), sign up for community college. If the idea is daunting, begin with just one class in a subject you enjoy. Complete 1-2 years' worth of community college classes at your own pace. Get decent grades.
- Apply to a 4-year college as a standard transfer student.

To see what this looks like in practice, consider the results of an informal online survey I conducted in 2017 of homeschoolers, unschoolers, and radical alternative school graduates who got into four-year college. Each respondent had an unique answer that depended on the colleges they were applying to, their state of residence, and their tolerance for hoop-jumping. Most used a combination of an unaccredited diploma, GED, standardized tests, and community college courses:

---

13 If your prospective college requires an accredited diploma, you can take the GED or HiSet, complete a state high school equivalency exam, or get an accredited diploma (from the Clonlara School or a similar program).

"I graduated this year from Portland State University with full honors, never having taken the SATs, ACTs, or completed more than a quarter of high school curriculum."

"We needed a high school diploma to apply for scholarships. It took a few tries; it's always best to ask administrators exactly what they are looking for. Each one wants something different and is often willing to show examples."

"For me, no diploma was necessary to get into four-year university. I had to take [the] ACT and provide them with a transcript which my parents had written up, signed, and sealed."

"I am in my last year at a university in England. When applying I only listed my associate degree from a community college (in Massachusetts) that I went to in place of high school. I also had a couple of references from professors and had to write one essay, but that was it. I started community college casually when I was 14 and gradually became full time. Neither my community college or current university ever asked for a GED or high school diploma."

"For my university applications my mom wrote a pretty extensive report about my activities throughout high school (helped by New York state's requirement to submit quarterly reports on 'homeschool' progress), the educational philosophy we used, etc. . . .I also took the SAT and ACT, had taken community college classes, and interviewed well, and maybe that would have been enough. But her report was like 14 pages and I bet it helped."

"I was able to enroll in Portland Community College without any documentation (I'm not sure if that's available to everyone or just people who are 18, which I was), so I got some credits under my belt while working on applications to transfer to 4-year schools. That included getting my GED and taking the ACT because of the requirements of the schools I wanted to go to. I chose to write an additional essay for my applications that 'explained' my application, because I didn't have many official records. I outlined unschooling and argued that my upbringing would be an advantage in higher education. When I later applied to graduate school, none of my applications required high school level documentation, just my undergraduate transcripts."

"I got into community college by talking my way in through their advisor for high school age students, taking a placement test, and saying I would get a high school diploma through my charter school before I graduated. (I technically didn't—I received it two weeks after I graduated.) Then all I needed to become an undergrad was to say I had an Associate of Arts degree from community college."

"I'm a current college student. I had an unaccredited transcript and SAT scores (the regular test, plus some schools required 2 SAT Subject Tests for homeschoolers). I also had some AP credits as well, but they weren't required for my applications."

"I went to a private university. To gain admittance I had to show my GED and write an entrance essay. That's it! It was shockingly easy."

"My GED from Pennsylvania was sufficient to get into an associate of nursing program at a community college in Arizona, and to the best of my recollection, nobody has ever really cared about anything before college since."

"My son is currently applying to a four-year university within the Maine state system. They told me they would accept either a traditional looking homeschool transcript or a narrative transcript. They do not require SATs or ACTs at this school for anyone. They do mention on their website that some homeschoolers may need to take the GED."

"Two of my children work for government-paid agencies and they required a high school diploma and accepted the one I created for them. Three went to community college and they accepted the diploma I made, as well as the very bare thread transcript I made (basically, a list of classes—titles only—and no grades were listed)."

"In Colorado I took a couple placement tests at the community college when I was fifteen and told them that I was homeschooled. They didn't ask for any kind of documentation of the homeschooling, or any high school diploma or GED. To apply [to a four-year, fairly competitive private university], I only had to provide my community college transcript, and they accepted me for this next fall as a transfer student with no request of ACT, SAT, or any mention of high school. They even awarded me the largest merit scholarship available, based on my community college grades."

"I got a homeschool diploma from Clonlara School in Michigan, which I set foot in maybe three times before

I graduated. . .After I took my first few [community college] courses, nobody has ever been interested in what I did in 'high school.' I transferred to a state school and now I'm like everyone else."

"I took the ACT and I think my parents created some type of diploma in Microsoft Word."

"I had an accredited high school diploma. Because I didn't have any grades, the four-year college I applied to refused to accept me to their Honors program, even with good SAT scores, a portfolio of academic work, and all A's in my community college classes. After a semester of straight A's, they invited me to join."

"In Oregon, my unschooled kids were eligible to take community college classes for credit without any proof of formal education. Passing the GED allowed them to apply for scholarships and financial aid, which they did. So far neither of them has needed to show proof of passing the GED outside of those financial benefits."

Community colleges play a vital role in helping unconventional students get into four-year college in the United States. By enrolling in community college at age 16 (or earlier), teenagers accustom themselves to college norms while also racking up the college credits that reassure apprehensive admissions officers. Some just take a few classes and apply as normal first-year students; others ramp up to full-time community college around age 18, obtain their associate degree, and apply as transfer students. In both cases, four-year institutions love seeing community college experience on the application of non-traditional learners.

If community college is inaccessible or undesirable for your kid, she can focus more on standardized tests. Colleges love seeing SAT, ACT, and SAT Subject Test scores in order to compare an applicant to her larger peer group. And fortunately, none of these standardized tests require attendance in conventional high school. All you need is a good test prep book and some dedicated time to fill in the gaps. The teens I've known have also employed YouTube, Khan Academy, formal textbooks, formal test prep courses, private tutors, family members, their peers, and the staff of alternative schools to prepare for such exams.

At this point you may be thinking: "Wow, it sounds like a kid needs to be really self-motivated to prepare for four-year college admissions. I fear the next ice age will arrive before my kid will willingly pick up a math textbook to brush up for the SAT."

This is a common fear, and it's a valid one. Now let me tell you what I've seen, time and again, working with teenage unschoolers and alternative school students. It's true that many of them show zero academic inclination, sometimes for years. They play Minecraft, they draw, they watch YouTube videos, they "mess around" and "do nothing" while you feel like you're watching a slow-motion train wreck. "How will my kid ever learn what they need for college?" You begin to wonder if your kid really should be slogging through math homework each night instead of crocheting, messaging friends, or racking up headshots in the newest first-person shooter video game.

Then, one day, your kid realizes that college may actually be a good idea. Maybe a few of his friends are going off to college. Maybe a YouTube idol inspires him to pursue a career that clearly requires a college degree. Maybe his Minecraft hobby spurs an interest in landscaping. Maybe he wakes up one day and realizes that he doesn't, in fact, want to live at home forever.

All of a sudden, for one reason or another, your kid finds a very personal reason to go to college—and this is the key that unlocks everything. All of a sudden, those community college placement exams don't seem so irrelevant. That SAT prep book doesn't seem so toxic. Khan Academy turns from enemy to friend. The GED turns from *some stupid test* into a *ticket out of here*. The academic coaching that you fruitlessly offered in the past turns into "Yes, mother, I would actually like to hear your advice. Yes, I would like your help with algebra. Yes, let's look for SAT prep classes together."

Sometimes this moment comes at the traditional age of 18; more often it unfurls at its own pace.

Artec Durham was a lifelong unschooler who grew up on his parent's wine grape farm in rural northern California. While both of Artec's parents had college degrees, they didn't pressure him to go to college, nor did they dissuade him. Artec didn't have a serious interest in academics, his parents didn't have money to contribute to his higher education, and he never took the SAT. At age 18 Artec spent most of his time working outdoor jobs while dabbling with part-time art classes in community college. He landed a summer job building trails as part of a Conservation Corps in Colorado where he eventually oversaw crews of college students and developed a budding interest in wilderness first aid. At 22, feeling ready to expand his horizons and pursue further training and credentials, Artec became a full-time student at Feather River College, a community college near his hometown.

"Being an older student in college led to so many opportunities," Artec told me. He signed up for an Emergency Medical Technician course where he immediately stood out as a motivated student. The instructor invited Artec to apply for a position at the local hospital emergency room, which soon led him to driving ambulances. Still living on a shoestring income, Artec paid for his ambulance driver's license entirely with coins at the DMV.

Working alongside doctors and nurses in the emergency room inspired Artec to tilt his career in the direction of medicine. He took prerequisite courses for nursing and then, at age 25, entered a four-year nursing program at Northern Arizona University. Again, Artec found that going to college as an older student with a clear purpose made college life much easier for him than it would have been at age 18. "It was easy for me to get A's because the other students didn't apply themselves," Artec recalls. He landed his dream job as a specialty intensive care nurse before he even graduated, thanks in large part to the work and leadership experiences he accumulated between age 18 through 22. And the cherry on top? He finished school with zero debt thanks to a combination of need-based and merit-based grants, including one designed specifically for older students.

Having faith that the moment will come where your kid spontaneously decides to catapult themselves into adult life is a cornerstone of unconventional education. We'll discuss how and why this moment arrives in further chapters. For the moment I'll just say this: the majority of homeschoolers, unschoolers, and radical alternative school students I've known—including those seemingly most opposed to structure and academics—do end up seriously considering college at some point between the ages of 16 to 20. If it seems right for them, they figure out how to get there. They grow up, get their act together, and jump through the hoops with surprising rapidity.

How They Get into Highly Selective Colleges

"That's all very nice, Blake. But it's not enough for my kid to get into any college—I need to know if they can get into the very best colleges."

Perhaps you're asking this question because you attended a highly selective college yourself, and it's scary to imagine your kid not following in your footsteps. Perhaps the terms *community college*, *GED*, and *unaccredited diploma* are triggering phrases for you, suggesting diminished economic prospects. Perhaps you simply don't want to restrict any of your child's opportunities, including the chance to attend an elite college.

No matter your concern, I will entertain it. College is the closest thing we have to a modern secular religion, and for many, going to an elite college is tantamount to walking through the gates of heaven. However flawed this belief may be—more on that in Chapter 5—I'd like to show you how unconventionally educated kids get into the most selective colleges, just to calm those nerves.

In 2019 I reviewed the homeschool admissions guidelines of the most selective universities in the United States:

NYU, Columbia, Dartmouth, the University of Pennsylvania (Penn), the University of California system, the University of Chicago, Duke, Johns Hopkins, Northwestern, Stanford, MIT, California Institute of Technology (Caltech), Harvard, Brown, Yale, and Princeton. Each differed slightly, but the overall message was clear. Here's what elite universities want from their non-traditional applicants:

- Evidence that you've pursued highly challenging academic work during your high school years
- A transcript that explains, in detail, the methods and content of your academic learning (it doesn't have to be accredited)
- Official transcripts from any accredited institutions you attended (like community colleges)
- SAT or ACT scores, plus two or more SAT Subject Tests (these are very important)
- Three letters of recommendation from those who have worked with the teen in a rigorous, face-to-face academic setting, like community college (no more than one should be from a parent)
- A personal essay that describes your motivations for homeschooling or for taking a non-traditional path, what resources you used, and how you took full advantage of your opportunities
- An in-person interview

The first thing to note is that virtually no elite universities require a high school diploma or GED, and the ones that do (like NYU) are okay with parents just creating their own diploma. So, it turns out that the one thing many people worry about—possessing an accredited high school diploma—doesn't matter much. What clearly *does* matter is doing challenging academic work, thoroughly documenting that work, doing well on standardized tests, writing well, and securing excellent letters of recommendation. Let's explore each of these.

First, highly challenging academic work. As Duke University put it, you should "take the best and most challenging courses available." These might include community college courses, dual enrollment courses, or online courses. Your studies should span the academic spectrum. Stanford wants to see "a serious, rigorous course of study distributed across the humanities, sciences, math, social studies and languages." Yale emphasizes that they "do not specify the number of years you must spend on any particular subject," as long as you're strong in "all the major disciplines."

Next, the self-created transcript. For any official courses you take, simply send official transcripts. For everything else—e.g., your online classes, home-brew science experiments, history lessons with the neighbors, National Novel Writing Month manuscript—you'll need to create a transcript that explains the content, methods, and evaluation criteria for each of your "courses." (You'll need to package each of your projects in the language of a formal academic course.) Some colleges want to see grades for your courses, along with an explanation of your grading scale; look at this is just another opportunity to explain your actual day-to-day methods and activities.

What else might you provide? Penn recommends "syllabi, lab work, reading lists, [and] textbooks," and NYU suggests bibliographies and syllabi. But the real message here is captured by Yale. "The more you can document for us and describe what you have done during your high school years, academically and otherwise, the better."

Standardized tests are typically non-negotiable for elite colleges. Almost all of them want an SAT or ACT score, plus two or three SAT Subject Tests. Northwestern requires that one of the SAT Subject Tests be math-oriented; that's strong advice no matter where you're applying. AP and IB test scores are welcomed supplements. For elite schools, standardized tests are far more valuable than subjective grades on a parent-crafted transcript. As a Cornell admissions representative said, "[We] have to put more emphasis on standardized test scores. . .[because] there would just be no way to trust [a homeschooler's] GPA and grades."

The final non-negotiable element is the personal essay. Elite colleges want to know the "why" behind your unconventional path. Penn asks: "What inspired you or your family to seek home schooling as an option for your education? Describe your curriculum in detail and tell us how you, your family, or oversight group has organized your pursuit of knowledge across core academic disciplines." Duke wants to know "why the student and family chose homeschooling, the setting for homeschooling, and the philosophy behind the education provided." Brown is curious about "the degree of liberty you have had in guiding your own education." Satisfy that curiosity!

One theme that consistently emerges is that selective schools want you to play well with others. Yale wants to see "evidence of social maturity from all our applicants and especially from home-schooled students. Your personal state-ment, interests and activities, and letters of recommendation should speak to your ability to integrate well with other stu-dents." MIT recommends participating in academic summer camp programs. Joining an undergraduate research team at a local university is another solid option.

The competition at top colleges is so intense that it helps to differentiate yourself with an outsized academic accom-plishment, such as winning a national competition. An unschooler from Mumbai, India got into MIT after winning three medals at the International Olympiad of Informatics; she's now studying computer science with a large scholarship.

But selective schools don't just want to recruit academics-obsessed robots. MIT says that "most of our homeschooled students have participated in extracurricular activities and community groups, such as community orchestras and theater, athletics groups, scouting, religious groups, volunteer work, work for pay, etc. Our homeschooled applicants, like all of our students, are active in their communities." Translation: be fabulous in one or two areas while also having a broad base of academic and non-academic experiences.

Show prospective schools that you've taken full advan-tage of your freedom and opportunities as a liberated learner. Here's MIT again: "One quality that we look for in all of our applicants is evidence of having taken initiative, showing an entrepreneurial spirit, and making the most of their opportu-nities. Many of our admitted homeschooled applicants really shine in this area. These students truly take advantage of their less constrained educational environment to take on exciting projects, go in depth in topics that excite them, create new opportunities for themselves and others, and more."

Antonio Buehler, a Stanford and Harvard graduate and the founder of Abrome, a small self-directed education center in Austin, Texas, plumbed the depths of the elite admissions process and concluded that "intellectual vitality" is the most important feature for unconventional teenagers to possess, because elite colleges are starved for young people with genuine passions and curiosities, instead of just those who are very good at *appearing* passionate and curious. Leaning on his prior experience as a college admissions consultant and volunteer for undergraduate admissions at Stanford and the United States Military Academy, Buehler understands the importance of passionate curiosity:

> While schools such as Harvard and Stanford can fill their classes many times over with valedictorians and applicants with perfect SAT scores, they cannot find enough applicants who have demonstrated that their love of learning extends beyond what they believe would benefit their college admissions prospects. Young people who get to pursue self-directed education can much more easily convey intellectual vitality simply by way of recounting how they poured themselves into their interests when they were free to choose how to spend their time. This gives them a tremendous advantage in the elite college admissions game.

Buehler even argues that intellectual vitality can even make up for poor grades, lower SAT scores, or especially strange homeschooling backgrounds.

What does this all look like in practice? Amelia Bryan

grew up in an eclectic homeschooling family. Her mom insisted that she and her brother do some amount of math, writing, and foreign language, and then asked, "what do you want to learn this year?"—and seriously followed their interests. Amelia danced ballet, wrote research papers about elephants, joined a theater group, learned French with Rosetta Stone, and studied biological anthropology with The Great Courses. Fortunate to be located near Village Home in Portland, Oregon (the "community college for homeschoolers" mentioned in the previous chapter), she took a range of classes but loved math and theater the most. Amelia always saw college in her future, and at age 14, her parents encouraged her to consider whether homeschooling or conventional high school would better serve her in this regard. Amelia opted to continue homeschooling, because then she could enroll in more challenging math classes. While completing two years of full-time community college classes (beginning at age 16), she also took the SAT (twice) and three SAT Subject Tests (Physics, Chemistry, and Math Level 2). She obtained strong letters of recommendation from two community college professors and a mock trial coach, and her mom put together an unaccredited homeschool diploma. Amelia applied to 14 colleges, including most of the Ivy League schools. Five offered her admission, five waitlisted her, and four rejected her. She ultimately decided to attend MIT for mechanical engineering, where she graduated in 2018, and then matriculated at Stanford Medical School.

If stories about young people like Amelia feel intimidating, recall the power of the community-college-and-transfer route. Keiran Healy was unschooled from fifth grade onward and only dabbled lightly in academics. She enrolled at a California community college at age 14, took five years of part-time classes (completing the general education curriculum required for transfer students), and applied at age 19 to four of the most selective members of the University of California system: Berkeley, Santa Cruz, Davis, and Los Angeles. Keiran got into all but Los Angeles, simply on the power of her community college record and the unaccredited homeschool transcript that her mom created. When I asked Keiran why she chose to attend Santa Cruz over (the relatively more prestigious) Berkeley, she told me, "I felt that I'd get more of the 'college experience' here at Santa Cruz. I don't think it matters where you go for your undergrad anyway. I mostly applied to Berkeley to prove that I could get in despite my informal education and show other people— scared homeschoolers, family, and any unbelievers—that homeschooling *does* work." So be it! Keiran is now on track to graduate from UC Santa Cruz in the Spring of 2021.

If you encounter seemingly impenetrable barriers when applying to a top school, always try talking to a human being before you give up. Elite colleges often grant audiences to potentially interesting and talented outsiders. The University of California system, for example, has a little-known policy called "admission by exception," which they explain thusly: "Sometimes even the most creative, focused and intellectually passionate students aren't able to fulfill our admission requirements. Even these students have a chance to attend UC." Begin a dialogue with admissions officers as early as possible. Tell them your story, demonstrate your motivation, find out what previously admitted students did to prove their mettle, and ask how you can give the college what they want to see.

Getting into a highly selective college can be an arduous game of achievement and posturing. You've got to simultaneously work your hardest, check all the right boxes, and somehow stay true to your intellectual curiosity. I've only known a handful of unconventional teenagers who opted for this path—but it has been walked, and your kid can walk it too, if they so choose.

How They Find Economic Security

Finally, we arrive at the question that lies at the heart of most parents' concerns about unconventional education: Will my kid be employable? Can they find economic security?

On one level, we've already addressed this concern by showing how young people get into college. Once your kid acquires a college degree, her unconventional upbringing simply becomes a non-issue. Employers don't care about a college graduate's high school diploma. She will simply compete for the same opportunities as all the other college graduates in this world.

What if she doesn't plan to go college, yet she wants a job that requires an accredited high school diploma? In this case, she can always take the GED or a similar high-school equivalency exam. I've seen many young people, including life-long unschoolers who consider themselves allergic to formal classwork, quickly do what's necessary to jump over these hurdles when they see that a desirable job is waiting on the other side.

In the U.S. we commonly assume that employers need to see an accredited high school diploma on a young person's résumé, and that the employer will actually expend the energy necessary to verify such accreditation. Yet many employers are content to see *any* high school diploma listed on a résumé, which means a diploma from a radical alternative school or a homeschool might work fine.

In my observation, unconventionally educated kids who choose not to attend college gravitate toward the arts, technology, and entrepreneurship—three broad fields where competency matters much more than credentials—as well as skilled trades and more commonplace service jobs. Gray and Riley's 2015 survey of grown unschoolers found a "remarkably high percentage" pursuing careers in the fine arts, crafts, music, photography, film, and writing. Entrepreneurs were also highly represented. Ken Danford's survey of North Star alumni revealed that the 34% who did not pursue traditional higher education were divided as follows: 20% went into ordinary work (e.g., restaurant work, landscaping, private childcare), 3% went into unusual work (e.g., professional circus work, music, theater, arts, work with animals), 5% worked for themselves, and 6% joined a certificate program, trade school, AmeriCorps, or the military.

Is it possible that an alternatively educated kid will mess around, waste their time, not learn much that society considers valuable, develop no interest in college, remain functionally unemployable, and end up living at home for a long time? Yes, it's completely possible. But I don't believe we should hold alternatively educated kids to an impossible standard. We should not resort to a cherrypicked fantasyland of unconventional learners who consistently go to Harvard, write best-selling novels, or start successful companies.

Instead, let's compare unconventional young people to their socioeconomic and geographic peers. Ask yourself, how many students from your kid's local school—the one they would be otherwise attending—end up messing around, wasting their time, and not learning much that society considers valuable? How many high schoolers develop no interest in college, remain functionally unemployable, and live at home for a long time? Very many do. This happens all the time. Conventional schools are not magic; they just make us feel comfortable by virtue of their conventionality.

Some young people simply need more time than average to grow up. Some kids aren't ready to begin their independent lives until sometime in their twenties. There is something to be said for nudging your fledgling out of the nest to help them learn to fly. There's also something to be said for waiting until they seem genuinely ready, milestones be damned. If your kid is going to "fail to launch" by societal standards, an alternative path may at least spare them the stress, anxiety, and torment of being prematurely and unnecessarily labeled a failure.

The kid you know today—the one who might seem angry, anxious, or anti-social—will not be the same person in five, ten, or fifteen years. Just as the most well-groomed Ivy-Leaguer-in-embryo can fall from grace, the seemingly hopeless school-hater can surprise you.

Jonah Meyer was one such kid. As a miserable sixth grader, he showed no interest in school now, or the possibility of college later, much to the chagrin of his middle-class parents. Unsure of what else to do, Jonah's parents supported him in dropping out of middle school and joining North Star, the self-directed learning center for teenagers we've encountered a few times now.

Given real control over his life, Jonah spent a few years focusing on his one love—rock climbing—and doing virtually nothing else that a typical parent would call productive. Yet one day, while casually browsing the science section of North Star's bookshelf, Jonah developed a budding interest in chemistry. He dove into the subject, reading everything he could, and soon reached the point where he had picked all the low-hanging fruit of chemistry knowledge. Then he discovered that the nearby University of Massachusetts Amherst offered an introductory chemistry course.

Jonah was aware that he was a middle-school dropout, but he also felt confident that he could succeed in this chemistry course. So he and his parents crafted a carefully worded email to the course's professor, kindly asking for permission for Jonah to audit, even though auditing was not formally allowed. They made it clear that Jonah didn't want to get credit for the course, he simply wanted to satiate his curiosity.

Touched by Jonah's email—because really, how many emails like this does a chemistry lecturer get each year?—the professor accepted the request. Jonah took the course, did fine, and walked away with a letter of recommendation from the professor.

Did Jonah continue his guerrilla education and go on to become a famous chemist? That would make for a compelling story, but no—Jonah's interests remained firmly in the outdoors. He ended up taking a one-year vocational training program in Outdoor Leadership at a local community college, which helped him get hired by the Wilderness School, a program run by the Connecticut Department of Children and Families (which apparently didn't mind his lack of high school diploma). For six years, Jonah worked with teenagers, led backpacking expeditions, and oversaw a climbing program, working intensively for half the year in order to save enough money to go on big, three- to four-month-long annual climbing trips in places like Norway, Sweden, Switzerland, and South Africa. In the remaining months of the year, Jonah worked odd jobs. Before his twenty-fifth birthday he learned what it was like to be a bartender, a bouncer, an EMT, a stagehand, a construction worker, and a route setter at a climbing gym.

Yet even after landing a plum job leading hiking trips in Washington's Olympic National Park, Jonah felt the need to move onto something bigger. He seriously considered getting a bachelor's degree in the sciences but ultimately decided on firefighting. When I caught up with him in 2019, Jonah was employed by a local firefighting department in Washington and about to begin attending fire academy the following week. In our conversation, Jonah took a moment to reflect upon his journey:

> One of the problems with our modern education system, I believe, is that we chunked everything up into unrelated subjects when the reality of the world says there is no such thing. I see this in my own story. It is very easy to break it up into parts and view it as a narrative of "wandering" and "searching" and "switching." Climbing. Chemistry. Outdoor education. Firefighting. I fall into this trap as well and often think of myself as constantly changing my mind and path. But when I actually look at my life and experience, I don't

feel that way at all. I feel like it has actually been a fairly logical path. My interest in the outdoors and adventure as a kid connected with my interest in science and chemistry, which helped me be a better outdoor educator; my experience in the outdoors handling challenging scenarios gave me the motivation and skills to join a fire department. What looks and often feels like a crooked path may actually not be so crooked. Everything I have done, I have learned from, and I have taken forward into the next thing I do. Society generally values people with diverse interests who have a demonstrated ability to thrive in different environments. And employers/colleges are willing and able to draw lines between your past experiences if you can communicate how your previous skills and learning apply to a new scenario.

Not long ago, Jonah was an angry and frustrated middle school drop-out. Today, he still doesn't hold a four-year college degree. Yet he has clearly found his own version of success. What this success will look like in five or ten years, we cannot say. I, for one, do not fear for Jonah.

In North America, and increasingly in other parts of the world, young people genuinely enjoy multiple roads to success. You don't have to force your kid to get a high school diploma at age 18, go straight to college, or perhaps even go to college at all. You can help them leave formal education, pursue their dreams on their own terms, and reenter the system if and when they are ready.

Notes

For practical resources related to this chapter—and every other chapter in the book—please visit the book's dedicated webpage: https://blakeboles.com/y/

"But Does it Work?"

In this chapter I don't share research on the outcomes of progressive schools, experiential schools, and virtual schools, because (1) many such programs end up resembling conventional college-prep high school in grades 9 and up (2) these organizations tend to be large enough to have conducted their own research, which you can discover yourself, and (3) it's the more radical approaches that *really* make people nervous, so I keep my focus on those.

The Colfax kids went to Harvard, Christopher Paolini wrote *Eragon*, and Billie Eilish won four Grammy awards. All were homeschooled. Does this say anything meaningful about homeschooling? For more discussion, see my blog post, "The Cherrypicking Caveat" (Dec 20, 2019). https://www.blakeboles. com/2019/12/the-cherrypicking-caveat/

How They Do in College

For an analysis of the comprehensive 2016 study published in *Educational Measurement: Issues and Practices*, see "College Performance: Homeschooled vs. Traditional Students" by Robert Lyon (May 22, 2017). http://icher.org/ blog/?p=3711

For Kunzman and Gaither's 2013 paper, see *Homeschooling: A Comprehensive Survey of the Research* (January 31, 2013). https://othereducation.org/index.php/ OE/article/view/10

Gray and Riley's 2015 survey of unschoolers can be found in full at "Grown Unschoolers' Evaluations of Their Unschooling Experiences: Report I on a Survey of 75 Unschooled Adults" and "Grown Unschoolers' Experiences with Higher Education and Employment: Report II on a Survey of 75 Unschooled Adults" in *Other Education: The Journal of Educational Alternatives* (2015).

Gray's comment about not being able to make "strong claims" about the general unschooler population is from "A Survey of Grown Unschoolers I: Overview of Findings" by Peter Gray (June 7, 2014). https://www.psychologytoday.com/us/ blog/freedom-learn/201406/survey-grown-unschoolers-i-overview-findings

The statistic "32% of adults holding bachelor's degrees in 2013" is from the NCES: https://nces.ed.gov/programs/digest/d17/tables/dt17_104.10.asp

The 1986 survey of Sudbury Valley School graduates by Peter Gray and David Chanoff is from "Democratic schooling: What happens to young people who have charge of their own education?" in *American Journal of Education* (1986).

https://www.self-directed.org/resource/gray-and-chanoff-1986/

The 1991 Sudbury Valley School graduate survey is from Daniel Greenberg and Mimsy Sadofsky's 1992 book, *Legacy of Trust.*

Ken Danford's survey of North Star alumni is from "What Happens to Self-Directed Learners?" (undated, accessed November 29, 2019). https://www.self-directed.org/what-happens-to-self-directed-learners/. Note that Peter Gray helped Ken design the study. The man is prolific!

The Circle School study is from "Circle School Graduates in 2015" (July 30, 2015). https://circleschool.org/wp-content/uploads/Circle-School-Grads-in-2015-July-30-2015.pdf

On the link between family income and SAT scores (and therefore college admissions), see "What College Admissions Offices Really Want" by Paul Tough (September 10, 2019). https://www.nytimes.com/interactive/2019/09/10/magazine/college-admissions-paul-tough.html

On what "better research" in the self-directed education world might look like, listen to my 2018 interview with Peter Gray on the Off-Trail Learning podcast. https://soundcloud.com/blakebo/peter-gray-on-the-evidence-for-self-directed-education

How They Get into College

My informal survey, which reflects both first-year students and transfer students from the past two decades who attended both public and private colleges can be found here: https://www.facebook.com/blake.boles/posts/10107601129163033 (I edited the responses for clarity.)

Artec Durham's story was obtained via personal communication in early 2020.

 How They Get into Highly Selective Colleges

The homeschool admissions guidelines for NYU, Columbia, Dartmouth, the University of Pennsylvania, the University of California system, the University of Chicago, Duke, Johns Hopkins, Northwestern, Stanford, MIT, California Institute of Technology, Harvard, Brown, Yale, and Princeton are easily found by googling "homeschool admissions [university name]." I was unable to find guidelines for Cornell, the University of Michigan, and UVA.

The Cornell admissions representative quote is from "Stanford, Cornell & Dartmouth Tell Mommyish How Those Homeschoolers Go Ivy League" by Lindsay Cross (August 20, 2012). https://www.mommyish.com/homeschoolers-go-ivy-league-359/

Some of the academic summer camps that MIT recommends include: Johns Hopkin's CTY, Duke's TIP, PROMYS, MathCamp, Research Science Institute, Tanglewood, and Interlochen.

The story of the Indian unschooler who got into MIT is here: "'Unschooled' Mumbai teenager Malvika Joshi makes it to MIT" (August 30, 2016). https://indianexpress.com/article/india/india-news-india/unschooled-mumbai-teenager-malvika-joshi-makes-it-to-mit-3003481/

Antonio Buehler's quote was obtained via personal communication in 2020. Don't miss his excellent article, "College Admissions for Alternative Schooled, Homeschooled, and Unschooled Applicants" (August 1, 2017). http://www.abrome.com/blog/2017/8/1/college-admissions-for-alternative-schooled

Amelia Bryan's and Keiran Healy's stories were obtained via personal communication in early 2020.

For more on the arduous game of achievement and posturing for highly selective colleges, see "Packaging your homeschooler for college admissions" by Penelope Trunk (September 21, 2016). http://education.penelopetrunk.com/2016/09/21/packaging-your-homeschooler-for-college-admissions/

How They Find Economic Security

The former high school teacher Wes Beach has successfully crafted unaccredited diplomas and narrative transcripts for unconventionally educated teenagers for decades, helping them secure lucrative jobs and admissions to selective colleges. Learn more about his process in his 2015 book, *Self-Directed Learning: Documentation and Life Stories*, and through his website, Beach High School. https://www.beachhigh.education/

Jonah Meyer's story was acquired via personal communication in 2019.

3: THEY STILL LEARN TO WORK HARD

Must We Do Work We Hate?

In order to encourage success, do we need to force kids to do work they don't like?

Even if your kid is suffering in school, even if you know that viable alternatives exist, and even if you can see that such alternatives have led other young people to successful adult-hoods—you may not feel convinced.

What if all those "other" kids you heard about—the homeschoolers and unschoolers and alternative-schoolers—are inherently smart and motivated, while your kid is more typical and unmotivated? (Perhaps he is even the *lazy* one who just wants to play games all day?)

What if that "moment" never comes: the one where your kid decides to finally study math to prepare for college admissions, to seek gainful employment, or to move out?

What if your kid decides that because they've never had to do anything they don't like, there's no point in starting?

These are valid concerns, and in the pages that follow, we will deal with them head-on. By the end of the chapter I hope you'll see that we can, in fact, let young people do things they find inherently interesting and pleasurable, and in their self-directed pursuit, they will discover that life's greatest rewards require focus, determination, and deferred gratification. They will learn these things because this is how life genuinely operates—and you are letting them live their own lives.

Inside many seemingly lazy and unmotivated young people is a powerful yearning to work hard and contribute to the world. It may be buried under school-inspired disillusionment—or under anxiety about seemingly insurmountable global issues like international strife or climate change—but it is there.

To Play Forever and Ever

In modern culture, the opposite of work is play. "Working hard" and "playing around" are oil and water. This is why we must convince kids to abandon their playful ways.

Peter Gray, whom we've already encountered a few times, begs to differ. Gray is a firm believer that young people don't need to be forced to work at all. What they *do* need is free play, all day. Parent-organized sports teams and playdates don't count. Through self-directed play, Gray proposes, children will accomplish all the learning and growing they need to become functional members of adult society. No forced labor required.

Gray's thesis is simple, provocative, alluring, and it gives us the perfect place to begin exploring how modern kids learn to work hard.

Gray began his academic career as a laboratory biologist researching rodent behavior. When his young son, Scott, started pushing back against school, Gray and his wife began seeking alternatives. They discovered the Sudbury Valley School, just a short drive from their home in Boston, enrolled Scott, and watched him thrive. Gray became fascinated with the school's methods and offered to conduct a survey of the school's graduates, which he eventually published in the *American Journal of Education*.

Inspired by this new line of research, Gray pivoted his career from biology to anthropology to study the child-rearing practices of early hunter-gatherer cultures (what some other researchers call "forager" cultures). He noticed that many foragers approached parenting and education from a sharply different angle than we do today: they seldom directed, controlled, or formally instructed their children. Instead, these forager parents let their children play most of the day. Gray noted how children in these cultures enjoyed access to the tools of their culture, played in age-mixed groups, and learned through direct observation of the adults at work in their society.

Gray drew a straight line between forager cultures and the Sudbury Valley School, where students received high levels of autonomy, played in mixed-age groups, and enjoyed access to the tools of their culture (e.g., books, computers, musical instruments). Just as forager children gained the skills they needed to contribute to their societies without coercion, Gray theorized, the students of free schools like Sudbury Valley gain the skills necessary to become functional members of a free and democratic society.

Today, Gray believes that any community that practices Self-Directed Education—a phrase he capitalizes to distinguish from everyday "self-directed learning"—necessarily prepares its young people for success. Through the non-profit he helped to found, The Alliance for Self-Directed Education, Gray promotes unschooling, democratic free schools, self-directed learning centers, and other approaches that give children maximum autonomy within a diverse, age-mixed community of children and adults.

Ultimately, Gray's argument is straightforward and powerful. As he summarizes it in his book, *Free to Learn*: "Children are designed, by nature, to play and explore on their own, independently of adults. They need freedom in order to develop; without it they suffer. The drive to play freely is a basic, biological drive." To the extent that this argument is true, it offers a powerful case for self-directed learning.

To Work Forever and Ever

Biologically speaking, Gray is correct to say that forager children and modern children are essentially the same. But how far does this analogy reach?

The anthropologist David Lancy offers a helpful counterpoint to Gray's sweeping thesis. Lancy's 2013 scholarly tome, *The Anthropology of Childhood*, explains how children's roles have evolved over time—and very much in response to changing societal conditions.

Forager societies were small, homogenous, and kin-based. Adult roles within these societies were few and largely prescribed by gender. Cultural change happened at a snail's pace compared to the modern world, and truly, forager children had just one life path to choose. (Do you want to become a forager just like your parents...or a forager just like your parents?) These children's lives also involved many obligations that we would call "work" today: fetching water, weaving, or caring for younger kids. The whole concept of childhood ended quite soon in forager culture, too—somewhere around age 13—at which point budding adolescents were thrust into very adult activities like game-hunting and childbearing.

Early societies and modern societies are clearly different, yet there's a broader lesson here. In every human society, Lancy observes, children start working as soon as they are capable of working. In pastoral societies, when an 8-year-old could effectively shepherd animals—that 8-year-old worked. In agrarian societies, when a 6-year-old could gather eggs or milk cows—that 6-year-old worked. In forager societies, if a young child could help hunt or gather, then they also worked—but it also happened that many young children did not work because they were not yet physically capable of contributing. If a young forager couldn't help stalk, kill, and clean a deer, then he was a liability on a hunting expedition. If picking a certain kind of berry required long arms, then a kid was better off hanging around the village. And this seemed to be the case. Until they became adolescents, many forager children were simply not able to contribute to the adult world.

From this point of view, perhaps foragers were not necessarily enlightened in their treatment of children. Perhaps they didn't value play for its own sake; play was just the easiest thing to let kids do until they grew up and could start working.[14]

---

14 Cross-cultural comparisons are always perilous, and I'm proposing one possible interpretation of the phenomenon of letting children follow their interests. Peter Gray's interpretation rests on the research of ethnologists who studied hunter-gatherer groups throughout the world and reported that these groups did not have a concept of work as "toil;" that all hunting and gathering was voluntary; and that hunter-gatherer egalitarianism made it wrong to tell another person what to do, no matter their age.

Adults across the ages have looked at children through the lens of their ability to meaningfully contribute to the world of work. If we look through this lens today, what do we see?

Worthless Kids

One of my favorite lines to deliver to parents in a public presentation is this: "Your kids are worthless." After a satisfyingly awkward pause, I then clarify that your kids—and everyone else's kids—have been rendered functionally worthless in modern economies in the sense that they're seldom able to produce anything of economic value. Most kids today simply wouldn't succeed in most adult jobs, and the jobs in which they could succeed are the ones we don't want them to do and have subsequently outlawed. (Child actors, athletes, musicians, and entrepreneurs do exist, but they are clearly the outliers.)

As John Taylor Gatto liked to say, if a young person doesn't feel useful to anyone, then they will feel truly useless. He was right. Young people today feel like they serve no function in the adult economy beyond their role as consumers.

I don't believe that adults have actively conspired to remove children's agency. Instead, it seems clear that the steady march of technological progress has eliminated or professionalized much of the repetitive labor that children performed since the agricultural revolution. In 1870, roughly half of the American population worked on farms; today, less than 2% does. And all those horrendous factory jobs? They've been automated or outsourced to less fortunate children in far-away countries.[15]

Modern kids are economically worthless because modern jobs require genuinely high levels of complex thinking and creative problem-solving—and also because modern jobs are far less accessible for direct observation. Gray observes this in one of his scholarly articles:

> For starters, we have reading, writing, and arithmetic—skills that were foreign to hunter-gatherers, as they did not have written languages and their ways of life required little if any numerical calculations. One might plausibly argue [...] that the three Rs, and perhaps some of the scientific ways of thinking that we value today, are sufficiently different from the skills that hunter-gatherers had to acquire that children would not learn through their natural exploration and play, no matter how prevalent and valuable the skills are in the society in which they are developing. Another obvious difference is that children in our society cannot observe, in their daily experiences, all of the ways that adults make a living. Our society is much more complex and less available to children than a hunter-gatherer society.

Regarding the three Rs, Gray goes on to argue that children who grow up "in a literate and numerate environment, in which they regularly experience the written word and numbers and interact with people who read and use numbers . . . indeed do learn to read, write, and calculate through their inherent curiosity and motivation to learn." On this I agree

---

15 Many children in recent generations did deliver papers, mow lawns, babysit, bag groceries, and take other part-time jobs. Those jobs still exist, but we don't let kids do them—a shift we can't blame on technology.

with Gray. I believe that this can extend to scientific ways of thinking, too.

But what about the observation problem? If you want to learn how to weave a basket, identify a plant, construct a temporary shelter, or track an animal, then you can genuinely "watch and learn" in the ways that forager children did. If, however, you want to design a better jet engine, become a talented human resources manager, or sell your art online to a niche audience, you'll need multiple years of training, on-the-job experience, or focused mentorship. Most middle-class knowledge work doesn't easily lend itself to apprenticeship or job-shadowing. Even when direct observation is feasible, liability concerns and labor laws often stand in the way.[16]

A forager child might have seamlessly transitioned into adult life because her childhood was essentially one long apprenticeship preparing her for one of the very few jobs available in her society. Modern young people, on the other hand, face a seemingly limitless number of jobs, many of which require advanced training, and few of which they can directly observe.

This is where the notion of unlimited free play can start to feel misplaced. If children need to gain complex skills—

---

16 Modern knowledge work is categorically different from agricultural work, factory work, or forager work—because knowledge work happens mostly in your head. For example, a kid can't watch a hedge fund manager at work in the office and really figure out what she's doing. But a kid can apprentice a blacksmith, because a blacksmith can work at her forge while being silently observed, take occasional breaks to explain what's happening and answer questions, and still get her job done. If a hedge fund manager took regular breaks to explain what she was doing, she would never accomplish anything.

and if their ability to observe and practice these skills through informal play is limited—then shouldn't they be doing something more "productive" with their time? Building abstract thinking skills, preparing for advanced training, and learning the ways of modern society? In other words, shouldn't they be doing school?

The Double Bind

The modern young person finds herself in a difficult situation.

She cannot effectively contribute to adult society, which is closed off to her, hidden behind office doors and laptop screens. She is aware that "good jobs" rely on genuinely complex skills, yet those skills only seem to be developed in college or specialized training programs that are many years away. The schoolwork that will supposedly prepare her for such advanced learning feels silly, inefficient, and only marginally relevant—as if she could mostly ignore it for years, return to it later when she's good and ready, and then knock it out quickly. (Her intuition is not wrong, in light of how many homeschoolers, unschoolers, and alternative school students do exactly this.)

Like all young people, she wants to have purpose. She wants to do things that matter. She wants to build skills and feel competent. She doesn't want to feel worthless and useless. She wants to understand the world and how she might contribute to it. But the only path before her is school, which feels suspiciously like a holding chamber.

As a parent, you may share this confusion. You want your kid to be prepared for twenty-first century work, but you have a hard time defining what exactly such work might be. You'd love for her to be able to directly observe adults at work—surgeons, biologists, event planners, building contractors—so that she might become genuinely motivated to pursue one of their paths, yet few such opportunities exist. You can't justify the importance of the schoolwork that your kid brings home, because most of it seems just as silly to you as it does to her.

On one hand, you think, there isn't much real work for your kid to do—so why force artificial work upon her? Let her learn, grow, and (yes!) play in her own way, all day.

On the other hand, the modern world is complex, and the competition is brutal—so how can you afford to ease up? If you let her do her own thing all day, isn't it possible that she'll wake up one day and realize that she's completely unprepared for the adult world?

At the end of his magnum opus, *The Underground History of American Education*, John Taylor Gatto warned against centering children's lives around "a slavish adherence to a utopian school diet of steady abstraction" or an "equally slavish adherence to play as the exclusive obligation of children." Is there a middle way? A way that embraces modern economic realities and the pleasures of play? A path that kids will voluntarily walk in their quest to become effective adults?

I believe that such a way exists, and it is best illustrated—curiously enough—by the phenomenon of modern video gaming. To prove this, I invite you to follow me a brief stroll down memory lane, after which we'll return to our larger discussion about work and play.

A Portrait of the Author as a Young Gamer

When I was 14, I fell in love—with a game.

The year was 1997, and the game was Diablo, one of the first online multiplayer role-playing games to hit the market.

In Diablo, your mission was clear: create a character, fight low-level monsters, gain experience points, and level-up. After reaching a certain level of proficiency, you would join a group of other players (usually total strangers) and venture underground to explore dungeons, fight bosses, find treasure, and level-up further.

Descending into a Diablo dungeon was no cakewalk. If my teammates and I didn't work together, we would get pummeled by beefed-up bosses with names like The Butcher, The Skeleton King, or Zhar the Mad. These underground quests demanded my full attention. Sometimes there wasn't even time to go to the bathroom, because 30 seconds away from the keyboard would spell certain doom. If we were fighting a big boss, dinner could certainly wait another 10 minutes. If I was facing Diablo himself, then good god, lock the door and don't talk to me for two hours! I had work to do.

Even though I never met my online questmates, I approached these missions with deadly seriousness. People were counting on me! I was needed! There was a mission to accomplish, one that I may have been working toward for weeks. Needless to say, I did not respond well to family members who accidentally picked up the phone and broke my dial-up modem connection.

Diablo was a wonderful game, but it wasn't my only love. As soon as I could pick up a game controller, I filled my life with video games, computer games, arcade games, tabletop role-playing games, and strategy card games. Notable highlights included The Legend of Zelda (age 5), Street Fighter II (age 9), Super Mario Kart and Dune II (age 11), Sim City 2000 and Final Fantasy VI and Magic: The Gathering (age 12—that was a big year), Star Wars: TIE Fighter (age 13), Dungeons and Dragons (age 14), Warhammer (age 15), Quake II (age 16), Marvel vs. Capcom (age 17), and Counterstrike (age 18).

Some of these games pitted me against computer-generated enemies, others against flesh-and-blood opponents. Some demanded intensive competition; others required careful cooperation. Some were expensive; others cost a quarter. Some were peaceable; others were violent. Yet not a single one of these games was ever *easy*. As soon as I mastered the game, that's when I would lose interest. The ones I loved most featured an endless series of obstacles, challenges, puzzles, and opponents with skills to match my own.

Despite their difficulty, my energy for gaming was seemingly limitless. After a long day of school, I would do my homework as quickly as possible, after which I dove straight into hours of intense gameplay. Weekends were reserved for marathon-length sessions of multiplayer games like Team Fortress Classic, sprawling role-playing game campaigns, or the occasional six-hour-long Magic: The Gathering tournament. Only at the point of sheer exhaustion—typically at some ungodly hour of the morning—would my friends and I press pause. If we could not focus, collaborate, or problem-solve, then we could no longer game. Our work was done.

The Work of Gaming

I came of age just as the modern gaming industry was blossoming in the 1990s. I didn't have the words to describe it then, but there was something special about these games—something that inspired me to dedicate entire afternoons, weekends, and summer breaks to tackling their difficult challenges. It's the same thing that prompts modern kids to throw themselves into Minecraft, Pokémon Go, The Sims, and Fortnite. And at the end of the day, it's the key to understanding how kids spontaneously embrace hard work.

But first: what is a game?

The game designer Jane McGonigal proposes that all great games possess four essential elements:

- Specific goals
- Clear rules that limit how you achieve a goal
- Feedback systems that tell you how close you are to achieving a goal
- Voluntary participation

Consider golf. The goal is simple: put the ball in the hole with as a few strokes as possible. The rules are simple: you must use golf clubs, you must play the ball where it lands, etc. The feedback system is clear: how close to the hole am I? And of course, golf is voluntary. No one forces you to play golf; we actually pay hefty sums for the opportunity.

All four elements of gaming are mandatory; remove one and golf ceases to be fun. If there were no rules, for example, then you could just pick up your ball, walk to the hole, and drop it in. If there were no feedback system—if you had no idea where you hit your ball—it would be a pretty sad game.

And if golfing were made mandatory then it would feel like middle-school physical education.

The word "fun" doesn't fully describe what's happening. Golf is only fun, for example, because the course is placed among a bunch of hills, sand, trees, and water between the starting position and the hole. Games are a "voluntary attempt to overcome unnecessary obstacles," in the words of philosopher Bernard Suits. The promise of endless challenge is what kept me in the dungeons of Diablo. The reward for finishing a quest in World of Warcraft isn't the end of the game; it's another, harder quest.

Games aren't just fun. They are, as Jane McGonigal puts it, "hard fun."

McGonigal's 2010 book, *Reality is Broken*, masterfully explains the psychology behind modern games. Many adults assume that it is a psychology of addiction, but look beyond Candy Crush and you'll see how unfounded that assumption is. (No compulsive gambler ever walked away from the casino having built a perfect replica of the Millennium Falcon, right? Thank you, Minecraft.)

Complex modern games give players a sense of personal ownership that psychologists call an internal locus of control: a state of mind that leads you to take responsibility for your successes and failures, instead of blaming them on outside factors. This is important, because as William Stixrud and Ned Johnson explain in *The Self-Driven Child*,

> Without a healthy sense of control, kids feel power-less and overwhelmed and will often become passive or resigned. When they are denied the ability to make mean-ingful choices, they are at high risk of becoming anxious,

struggling to manage anger, becoming self-destructive, or self-medicating.

Great games also generate the mental state that psychologist Mihaly Csikszentmihalyi famously called "flow." When you're in a flow state, you're tackling a perfect challenge: one that pushes you just beyond your skill level, demands total concentration, and offers continuous feedback. Csikszentmihalyi's research was based on high-level chess players, basketball players, rock climbers, partner dancers, and surgeons at work—but modern gamers clearly fit the bill. Those in a flow state don't notice the passing of time, may neglect basic needs like eating and urination, and otherwise seem to lose themselves in the activity. (Sound like anyone you know?)[17]

McGonigal highlights one more crucial feature of many modern games: their incredible sociality. Long ago, if your kid played Super Mario Brothers in the basement all weekend, you might rightly fear for their social development. Today, games like Fortnite are the new social hubs, as the novelist Keith Stuart explains in a brilliant essay entitled "Fortnite Is so Much More Than a Game":

---

17   To be clear, I'm not making the case for unlimited electronic gaming. McGonigal's research suggests that young people will reap positive benefits from gaming up to 20 hours a week–that's about 3 hours a day–but beyond 40 hours a week, "the psychological benefits have disappeared entirely and are replaced with negative impacts on your physical health, relationships, and real-life goals." McGonigal also recommends playing with real-life people instead of online strangers; playing cooperative games more often than competitive games; and choosing games that encourage design and creation (like Minecraft) over more mindless alternatives. Even the most radical of unschoolers would agree with McGonigal's final advice: "Any game that makes you feel bad is no longer a good game for you to play."

For my sons and a lot of kids their age, Fortnite is not a game they play, it's a place they go—and, importantly, it's a place they go with friends and not with Mom and Dad. It's fulfilling the same development role as those illicit teen spaces from the 1970s and '80s—those dodgy youth clubs, arcades, and video stores that we discovered unchaperoned. . .People who don't play Fortnite, or video games in general, often say it's sad that modern teens aren't going to skateparks and roller discos and that they're getting these formative experiences online instead. In some ways, I guess it is, but kids aren't necessarily to blame here. Teenagers are caught in a crappy sociocultural Catch-22: Adults are worried their kids are spending too much time on smartphones and consoles, but at the same time they're constantly policing and restricting access to physical environments.

Peter Gray makes a similar point in *Free to Learn*:

When kids are asked, in focus groups and surveys, what they like about video games, they generally talk about freedom, self-direction, and competence. In the game, they make their own decisions and strive to meet challenges that they themselves have chosen. At school and in other adult-dominated contexts they may be treated as idiots who need constant direction, but in the game they are in charge and can solve difficult problems and exhibit extraordinary skills. In the game, age does not matter—skill does. In these ways, video games are like all other forms of true play. Far from contributing to the general rise in anxiety, depression, and helplessness, video games appear to be a force that is helping to relieve those afflictions. This seems to be especially true in recent times, with the emergence of so-called massively multiplayer online role-playing games, such as World of Warcraft, which are far more social than previous video games and offer endless opportunities for creativity and problem solving.

Modern games are challenging. They give kids a sense of control. They lead to flow states. And many are highly social. This is a package deal that's hard to find elsewhere in life, and that's why kids will work incredibly hard on games with zero prodding.

Now let's tie it all together.

- The modern economy—like many forager economies—makes it very difficult for young people to meaningfully contribute.
- At the same time, modern young people—like young people of every era—want to contribute, build skills, and become effective adults in the world. They want to feel useful, not useless.
- The role that we have given kids today—to work full-time in school—feels empty, irrelevant, and wasteful to many of them. They sense that it's a rigged system that doesn't actually prepare them for adult life.
- These kids rightly reject the game of school and flock toward better games: ones where they actually learn, grow, collaborate, and develop complex thinking skills.

We adults have got gaming totally wrong. Games are not

the antithesis of work; games *are* work.[18]

"Games make us happy because they are hard work that we choose for ourselves," McGonigal summarizes, "and it turns out that almost nothing makes us happier than good, hard work."

The Magic of Intrinsic Motivation

Well-designed games like Fortnite, Minecraft, and The Sims offer vivid examples of how kids will happily challenge themselves, but the underlying principle goes far beyond electronic gaming. Recall our earlier question: is it possible for kids to take a middle path that both prepares them for modern work and embraces free play?

If we take McGonigal's definition and cast our gaze beyond the world of gaming, the answer quickly appears. Our world is filled with activities for young people that feature specific goals, clear rules, useful feedback, voluntary participation, and (ideally) lots of social interaction.

Within the realm of conventional school there's drama, band, mock trial, sports teams, and robotics teams: the activities that make school "worth it" for so many students. In the after-school world, it may be dance, gymnastics, parkour, skateboarding, or martial arts. During the long summer

---

18 To what extent are conventional schools game-like? They do possess goals, rules, and feedback systems. But their compulsory nature clearly separates them from the kind of games I describe positively in this book. Two interesting implications follow: (1) unconventionally educated young people have a big potential advantage when they voluntarily choose to attend conventional school, because they can better look at it as a game, and (2) if we made conventional schools more like college, letting students choose their own classes and study methods, I suspect school would feel more like "hard fun" than mere drudgery.

hours, young people may care for horses, build treehouses, produce their own movies, or go on backpacking trips. None of these activities are games, formally speaking, but they share the characteristics of great games. Each presents a difficult challenge that a young person undertakes voluntarily because they want to build skills, feel a sense of belonging, and do something meaningful with their time.

Another good way to describe this phenomenon is with the psychological concept of intrinsic motivation.

Most people use this term synonymously with "self-motivation," but it's a bit more nuanced than that. According to self-determination theory, humans have two basic motivation drives: intrinsic and extrinsic. To be intrinsically motivated is to do something for its own sake, not as a means to an end. Developing meaningful relationships, building skills, and feeling like you're contributing to a cause are classic examples of intrinsically motivated activities. The rewards of such activities are resilient; other people cannot easily take them away from you. Extrinsic rewards, on the other hand, have short shelf lives, and they're usually contingent on factors outside your control. Money, grades, body image, social hierarchy—such things come and go.[19]

---

19 I'm presenting a simplified breakdown of intrinsic versus extrinsic motivation here for the sake of brevity. The varieties of extrinsic motivation are actually quite nuanced, manifesting as different types of regulation. "External" regulation is heavy-handed control, pure and simple. "Introjected" regulation describes internalized beliefs (e.g., I must get good grades in order to succeed) of which someone isn't aware. "Identified" regulation is when someone can name their extrinsic motivators, even if they don't agree with them (e.g., when an unschooler decides to attend community college). "Integrated" regulation is when someone fully accepts an extrinsic motivator (e.g., when a video gamer embraces the fact that they're playing for virtual gold coins). Extrinsic motivators of the "identified" and "integrated" variety are not actually threatening to intrinsic motivation.

In the world of self-directed learning, we are quick to glorify intrinsic motivation and vilify extrinsic motivation. But as the author Daniel Pink explained in his 2008 book, *Drive*, both motivational drives are important for human success. Extrinsic motivation helps us do tedious and unsavory work, like cleaning a bathroom. Intrinsic motivation helps us accomplish more creative, complex, and meaningful tasks, like redesigning a bathroom. And because so many of today's job opportunities fall within the creative/complex realm, intrinsic motivation is the predominant drive for gainful employment in the twenty-first century.

Yes, there are still mindless and repetitive jobs in the world, Pink concedes. But these jobs have been leaving the developed world for decades—thanks to technology and globalization—and they're not coming back. Appearing in their place are two new types of work: high-tech (in which humans work alongside smart machines instead of competing against them) and high-touch (in which we humans take advantage of our unique capabilities for design, storytelling, big-picture thinking, and empathy).

Search online for the U.S. Bureau of Labor Statistics' list of fastest growing occupations and you'll see a mix of high-tech and high-touch occupations: computer programmers, wind turbine service technicians, home health aides, occupational therapists, and nurse practitioners. Some of these jobs are higher paid, some are lower paid, but they all share one common feature: none can (yet) be done better by a robot, software application, or foreign worker.

This is why I believe games and other self-chosen activities—by which I mean, "hard fun" activities with specific goals, clear rules, continuous feedback, and voluntary participation—equip young people to succeed in the modern economy. Whenever a young person chooses to do a challenging activity for herself, she is exercising her capacity for intrinsic motivation. The specific activity doesn't matter much as long as she is fully engaged, working alongside others, and pushing past obstacles. These are the transferable skills that will lead her to a high-tech or high-touch career.

You don't have to force your kid to do work she hates in order to succeed in this world. When she has a clear reason for doing her work, she will be far more likely to embrace its unsavory aspects. When she looks at work as an interesting game, she'll be more excited to wake up and push forward each day. There's no reason that any of this must wait till age 18. Pursuing hard fun can become your child's primary occupation, beginning this very moment.

How to Engage a Teenager

When a child is playing, we adults should try hard to not interfere. Play is a child's work, and you wouldn't like it if someone kept interrupting your work, would you?

This is a common argument in the world of self-directed learning, and it applies splendidly to young children. In adolescence, however, I don't believe we can place absolute faith in the power of free play.

Adolescents are not the same as children. They are different people with different needs and inclinations. When someone observes that a 5-year-old enters elementary school with a love of learning that fades in middle school, then school may deserve some (or much) of the blame. But isn't it also possible that a 5-year-old's wide-eyed curiosity will naturally evolve into something else? Without the institution of school, would every single person retain their passionate, playful, child-like curiosity through adulthood and old age? I don't buy it. Stage theories of development hold *some* water, even after removing conventional school from the picture. A child raised by conscientious unschooling parents can still become a surly, disaffected, and seemingly uncurious adolescent.

There is a blurry line between childhood play and adult work that the advocates for unlimited free play don't address—and this blurriness holds many parents back from supporting educational alternatives that could otherwise help their kids.

Engaging a young child is straightforward; let them play. Engaging a teenager is trickier. Teens are peer-oriented, not adult-oriented. They're curious about the hidden rules of the social world. They're beginning to consider their long-term futures. They're prone to adult-level anxiety and depression. And despite appearances to the contrary, I believe that every adolescent desperately wants to become an effective adult, to escape the powerlessness of childhood.

So how do you help a teenager become intrinsically motivated? How do you encourage them to voluntarily undertake challenges? How do you nurture a love for "hard fun?" How do you get a teenager to gain skills and a work ethic, not by tricking them, but by fulfilling their genuine needs?

My career has centered around these questions. At age 21, I made a commitment to myself: I would only work in places where youth voluntarily *chose* to be. I would not lend my labor to places of coercion. I also loved being in nature and wanted to work outside whenever possible. This led me to employment in the fields of outdoor education and summer camps, where I lined up back-to-back work seasons in my early twenties. At 25 I created my little company, Unschool Adventures, and began offering longer-term travel and retreat programs for unschooled and otherwise self-directed teenagers. In each of these environments, I witnessed young people—conventionally schooled, alternatively schooled, and unschooled—enthusiastically embrace challenges, build skills, and rapidly mature.

In this section, I share the practical details of what I've done and learned along my journey in the hope that you'll find some nuggets of inspiration for your own teenagers, your future teenagers, or the other young people whom you serve.

The Adventure Semester

How do you inspire teenagers to do hard things that lead to growth? In 2015, my friend Dev Carey and I co-designed and co-directed an Unschool Adventures program that explored that very question. We called it the Adventure Semester.

Dev and I brought together 23 teenagers and five staff for 10 weeks, spending the first five weeks on Dev's property in rural Western Colorado, just outside the town of Paonia. We organized the teens into groups of four or five, and every day we assigned each group a unique "adventure" that was facilitated by a specific staff member. The groups rotated through each adventure, so every teen eventually experienced every challenge. In the evenings, the groups gave brief presentations to the whole community about how their day went, regardless of whether they succeeded or failed. The next week we mixed up the groups, created a brand-new set of adventures, and did it all over again.

Here are a few of our one-day adventures, which the teens had roughly six hours to complete:

- UNSEEN: Sneak from one side of town to the other without being seen by anyone.
- MAPMAKING: Interview residents of Paonia and create a themed map (e.g., a dog owner's guide to Paonia) that would be printed and distributed at a local festival.
- MEDITATION: Wake up before dawn, hike together to a local hill in the woods, choose your own spot, and sit silently for five hours.
- MAKEOVER: Consider how you present yourself to the world (dress, appearance, and personality) and attempt a complete makeover for the day.
- WEB DESIGN: Choose a domain name, install WordPress, and create a basic, professional-looking website that represents you to the world.
- TEACHING: Teach a basic skill (like knot-tying) to others with restricted vision (blindfold), hearing (soundproof earmuffs), and mobility (wheelchair).
- BIRDHOUSE: Build a functional birdhouse out of junk material.
- COUNTER-ARGUMENT: Take a controversial subject that you have a clear opinion on, research the opposing side, and attempt to discredit your original beliefs.
- COLLEGE: Spend the day at Western Colorado University; talk to students and professors, sit in

on classes, use the library, and speak with admissions officers.

- ENTREPRENEURISM: With $20 seed funding, generate as much money as possible using only your group's preexisting skills and wits.
- BUILD A FIRE: Start a fire over which you'll cook lunch—no lighter, matches, or flint allowed.
- LISTENING: Engage strangers in Paonia over controversial issues, making use of deep listening skills.
- PERSEVERANCE: Choose a repetitive physical skill and practice it for six hours, pushing through your resistance to the activity.
- EMAILS: Compose and send two important types of email: a request for a letter of recommendation and a request to interview an interesting stranger.
- FOOD: Prepare breakfast, lunch, and dinner for the entire Adventure Semester.[20]

Some weeks we switched things up and offered two-day-long challenges, including:

- ENGINEERING: Figure out how to move a 5,000 lb. boulder six feet.
- CLIMBING AND RUNNING: Wake early to climb Mount Lamborn (11,000 ft.) on day one; practice trail running and wilderness first aid scenarios on day two.
- MURALING: Compose an original mural inside one of the bunkhouses.

---

20 The "food" challenge was the only recurring one—this is how we ate! One week the food group even butchered their own chickens.

- 48-HOUR THEATER: Rehearse and perform a play for a dinner audience.
- MINIMALIST CAMPING: Sleep overnight in the woods with only five items per person.
- D.I.Y. ROAD TRIP: Design a two-day road trip in Colorado using only recommendations from locals you meet along the way—no guidebooks or internet research.
- ONE RED PAPERCLIP: Trade a paperclip to a stranger for something of greater value, and then trade that, and so on.

Eventually we had the teens design their own multi-day challenges. They purchased thrift store t-shirts and screen-printed shirts for the entire Adventure Semester group. They reupholstered a couch. They created a yearbook and prom dance and original horror film. One group even decided to lock themselves in a room for 32 straight hours with each other, just to see what would happen. (Yes, they had a bathroom. Yes, we delivered meals to them. No, nothing horrible transpired.)

On week six, we shifted the main location to the town of Crested Butte—in order to offer challenges that required the resources of a larger community—and then in the final week, we migrated again to downtown Denver. There we sent our groups on adventures that directly related to the challenge of beginning an independent life in a big city: they inquired about room rentals, handed résumés to employers, and met with interesting adults whom they'd previously cold-emailed. We also had some fun. On the very last day of the Adventure Semester, for example, we custom-designed adventures for specific groups of teens. I blindfolded three of the musically inclined teens, drove them to nearby Boulder (45 minutes away from Denver), removed the blindfolds, and left them on the streets with only their cell phones, their musical instruments, and their challenge for the day: earn enough money through busking to get yourself back to Denver before dinnertime. They had seven hours to do this. They returned to Denver on a public bus with two hours to spare.

By everyone's account, the Adventure Semester was a success. The teens involved worked incredibly hard on a bunch of wacky challenges. They learned and grew. I'm not suggesting, however, that you need some elaborate program in order to engage a teenager. To me, the Adventure Semester offers concrete representations of the broad principles that turn "hard" into "hard fun." Every adventure had clear goals, rules, and feedback systems. The adventures were more often social than solitary. We adults didn't come up with a pre-set 10-week curriculum; we crafted our challenges week-by-week, based on the personalities and performance of the actual teens in our care. To the extent that you put these principles into practice—or find other people that do—you'll find equal success.[21]

---

21 In the self-directed learning world, there's an interesting and ongoing tension between consent and commitment. On the Adventure Semester, for example, we didn't allow teens to casually opt-out of adventures, except when they were sick. But we also made sure that every participant knew what they were signing up for before they were allowed to join the program; no one's parents were allowed to just "sign them up."

Real Work

When seventh grader Marc Gallivan was in conventional school, he cleaned the erasers in his math class every day. This wasn't punishment; Marc volunteered for eraser duty because he wanted to feel useful. Two years later, Marc joined Alpine Valley School, a nearby democratic free school that followed the Sudbury model. As someone who liked to contribute, a world of opportunity had burst open:

I looked at the list of available Clerkships [and] my eyes grew wide. My heart leapt as I read about jobs like Grounds Clerk (caring for the school grounds), Building Maintenance Clerk (caring for the building itself), Elections Clerk (handling all electoral functions at school) and so forth. These were important positions that contributed to the well-being of the school and I could nominate myself for any one of them. Some, like Building Maintenance Clerk, I was clearly unqualified for as a fourteen-year-old who was much better at banging my finger with a hammer than actually pounding a nail. But others, like School Meeting Chairman, or Judicial Clerk, were a natural fit. My first year at AVS I nominated myself for many positions, and [I] was elected to nearly all of them by School Meeting. Then the real work began.

Conventional schools seldom offer students the chance to assist in day-to-day operations. The one role that a young person is allowed to play is that of student. Alternative schools like Alpine Valley, on the other hand, offer kids a hundred ways to be genuinely useful. A kid who feels useful will seldom feel useless.

Outside of such special environments, how can parents

and young people find opportunities for real, meaningful work? Formal apprenticeships and internships for adolescents are rare today, but you can create your own. Homeschooler Jenny Bowen, age 15, brought her exotic white mice to the (one-and-only) exotic animal clinic in Wichita, Kansas. She hit it off with the veterinarian and, with her mother's assistance, proposed an informal apprenticeship. The vet said yes, and soon Jenny was helping to tube-feed parrots, neuter rabbits, and remove rat tumors. She delivered specimens to the local university, and she assisted with retail sales and booking appointments. After a year of faithful service, the vet decided to give Jenny the keys to the office and started paying her a small stipend.

Your kid will undoubtedly need your assistance to create an apprenticeship or internship out of thin air. Help them grasp the *quid pro quo* nature of such arrangements—how it's not just one-sided. I've coached many teenagers navigating this process, and they always find it engaging, I suspect, because they are learning how to navigate the social and economic worlds, how to negotiate, and how to make something "real" happen.

Traditional jobs are great options, too. According to Ken Danford, many of the 16- to 18-year-olds at North Star happily take entry-level jobs—at Walmart, McDonald's, or washing dishes—to earn spending money. Some teens enjoy these positions, and the ones who don't are often motivated to explore more entrepreneurial ventures like yard raking, cake baking, or dog walking.

Wilderness

When I was 11, I went on my first two-night overnight backpacking trip at Deer Crossing Camp. My love for the wilderness blossomed, and each summer I embarked on progressively more challenging trips, culminating at age 15 with the Ascent trip—an off-trail adventure that a small group of campers planned and led entirely on their own. Two Deer Crossing instructors trailed the Ascent group through the wilderness, acting as a sort of insurance policy in case someone got injured or the entire group got hopelessly lost. Fundamentally, the instructors' mandate was to remain mostly invisible and let the young people run their own trip, for better or worse.

I thoroughly enjoyed my Ascent trip at age 15—my group abandoned our ambitious itinerary to laze around some natural waterslides for two days—but the real fun took place when I returned to work at Deer Crossing while in college and just after graduating.

"Fun" is a relative term here. On the six Ascent trips I helped run, I spent a mind-boggling amount of time watching 15-year-olds attempt to hike through dense brush, waste precious daylight with lazy lunch breaks, and debate over navigational decisions that seemed shockingly obvious to me. ("Where is the trail?" The trail is literally *right there* in front of you.) It was tough to keep my mouth shut, but it was worth it to watch the gears turn and the growth happen. There were entertaining moments, too, like when a group confidently completed a map-and-compass analysis and then proceeded to walk in the *exact* wrong direction.

I especially cherish the memory of one Ascent group that

was excited for the grand feast of macaroni and cheese they planned for the first night out. They had successfully remembered to bring the pasta, the stove, the cooking fuel, and the cutlery…but as they had rushed out the door at 6 a.m., they had forgotten to double-check whether anyone packed a cooking pot.

As the sun set over nearby Highland Lake, nearly 8000 ft. in elevation, the teens were unpacking their bags and soon realized their great oversight. No cooking pot. They peered over at me, one of the two "ghost" instructors who had been following them all day. I was warm and toasty in my sleeping bag, boiling up my own pot of macaroni and cheese in my personal cooking equipment. They oh-so-graciously asked if they might borrow my cooking pot after I'd finished dinner.

"Sorry," I replied. "This is the Ascent." No cooking pot for them.

They ate Clif Bars for dinner.

Was this a tough moment for these teens? Yes. Did they survive? Yes. Would any of them *ever* forget to check their gear before departing for a wilderness trip again? No way.

Ascent trips were packed with suffering. Campers wasted time, argued endlessly, scraped themselves up, and dealt with temporary hunger. Yet universally, when they returned to camp after three days, they were overjoyed with a sense of accomplishment, having completed their first "solo" trip in the backcountry.

There is a reason why outdoor adventure programs like Outward Bound have consistent success engaging adolescents: nature is a wonderful teacher because its boundaries are wonderfully real. On a wilderness trip, you truly have to care for yourself. If you get injured, they'll send for the helicopter, but it might not arrive soon enough. If you run away unprepared, you probably won't last very long. If you forget a vital piece of equipment, you have to navigate the consequences of your decisions and oversights.

Just a century ago, the typical 15-year-old was helping on family farms, working for other people's businesses, caring for siblings, piloting vehicles, raising animals, and perhaps even starting their own family. Teenagers faced real boundaries, day after day. Wilderness offers teens a taste of the "real world" where boundaries have consequences.

There are a hundred ways to engage a kid with wilderness, from a weekend expedition in their local area, to forest kindergartens, to multi-month adventures like Kroka Expeditions' "Arctic to Manhattan Semester" where teens ski and paddle 750 km from Quebec to New York City. For low-cost and no-cost wilderness opportunities, google the idea of microadventures, popularized by British adventurer Alastair Humphrey.

Travel

Many teenagers want to travel, yet few do because (1) they have no time, (2) they have no one to go with them, and (3) travel is expensive. Choosing an unconventional educational path frees up time. Joining an alternative school or other community offers companions. And about money— well, you simply don't need to go half-way around the world and spend gobs of money to enjoy a travel adventure. That's what I learned from John Taylor Gatto, who sent his middle school English class students into five boroughs of New York City to interview businesspeople, survey strangers, rate public swimming pools, create maps, and lobby politicians. Gatto offered the essential experience of independent foreign travel to adolescents by helping them see their own land with a new sense of possibility.

Don't get me wrong—I adore foreign travel. I love how effortlessly and automatically self-directed learning happens when you're struggling with language barriers, getting lost on public transport, or you simply need to feed yourself. When I ran Unschool Adventures trips in foreign countries, I tried to give my teen groups large amounts of free time each day. They didn't need me to carefully plan out every hour of their time; that would have actually been detrimental. Instead I created a safe foundation for them—I booked the hostels, arranged the buses, made sure they got fed, and organized a few group activities—and they took care of the rest with their intrinsically motivated explorations.

Youth travel programs are always expensive, but keep in mind that it might just take *one* big travel adventure to create a life-long transformation. Milla von Tauber, a 16-year-old from Georgia who had just quit school, joined my six-week Unschool Adventures trip to Nepal in 2014. Some of the other teens showed Milla the basics of blues-style partner dancing on the roof of a Kathmandu hostel, which she immediately loved. After the trip Milla got involved in her local dance scene, started traveling to regional dance events, and now she dances, teaches, and performs all over the United States.

The Nepal trip cost Milla's family $4,500 plus another $2,000 for airfare, lunches, and spending money. $6,500 for a six-week adventure? It's certainly outside the budget of most families—but this was also a special, one-time expenditure.

Spreading the cost over three years, her family needed to save $2,200 a year to make that adventure happen; still a lot of money, but within the realm of feasibility for a middle-class American family.

Group Living with Strangers

At home, children occupy their little fiefdoms. They are comfortable and catered to, which often leads to parent-child conflicts about their bad habits and antisocial tendencies. But fundamentally, you are not going to kick them out, because you are their parent and you love them. (This is a good thing.)

When your kid lives under someone else's roof, however, their bad habits are quickly noticed and challenged. Imagine an overnight summer camp, a family homestay in Spain, or a boarding school. In each case your offspring is cared for by other adults whose mission is to keep him safe, happy, and engaged. At the same time, these adults must ensure the health and sanity of the overall community. So if your child is making other people miserable through his careless actions, he will hear about it. If he doesn't pull his weight doing chores, he will hear about it. If he leaves a mess in a host family's kitchen, he will hear about it.

The best sleepaway camps, boarding schools, homestays, and adventure programs never shame, demean, or physically punish a kid. They use nonviolent communication, restorative justice, or other humane approaches for delivering feedback. But deliver it they shall, and if your kid doesn't respond to that feedback, he will be sent home.

This is why group living with strangers can be incredibly empowering. I think of the Writing Retreat: a month-long residential program for around 20 teens that Unschool Adventures offered for many years. Ostensibly, the Writing Retreat was about helping self-directed teenagers complete an ambitious, self-assigned writing challenge. But after running this program a number of times, I saw that the biggest benefit came from teens living together in close quarters (typically 4 to 6 to a dorm room). They cooked, cleaned, socialized, and wrote alongside each other for a full month. A small group of staff members kept things in order but otherwise left the teens to do their own thing. The magic took care of itself.

Almost any extended overnight experience can offer similar magic. But it must be overnight, and it must be more than just a few nights. When such experiences are short-term, kids can hide who they are and hide what they think of others. With extended time together, people see all sides of each other—the sleepy side, the grumpy side, the elated side—and these are the building blocks of real connections, real relationships, and a real sense of community.

All-in-One Programs

Tucked away in a quiet corner of Western North Carolina, the Arthur Morgan School (AMS) is a Montessori-influenced Quaker boarding school that serves 27 students, aged 12 to 15 years old.

Here, the kids do everything: They chop the wood that heats the buildings, cook and serve the meals, do the laundry, maintain the property, farm the food (which they'll later eat), build the fences, and sometimes even assist with plumbing and electrical repair work. AMS students live in five-person, consensus-run, family-style homes, where they live, play, and work together under the supervision of two "houseparents" who are also teachers. While AMS does have compulsory academics, the classes are small and focused on interdisciplinary themes rather than conventional subjects, with a heavy emphasis on social justice and hands-on, real world applications. Students also have access to a plethora of music, theater, and art spaces, including a blacksmithing forge, ceramics studio, photography dark room, and fiber arts studio. Each week the entire AMS community comes together for an all-school meeting where students can influence the school's curriculum, rules, and budget. Students also participate in small committees to plan events, raise money for causes, or create public art installations. Finally, there are the adventures. Every year at AMS, students go on at least four trips, including a three-day wilderness backpacking trip, a six-day wilderness backpacking trip, and an eight-day backpacking, canoeing, or biking trip. The final trip, a co-created 18-day road trip, revolves around a central theme like coastal ecology, civil rights, or robotics.

Group living, travel, real work, and wilderness: the Arthur Morgan School combines so many engaging elements that I felt compelled to create a section just for them, the "all-in-one program." The trouble is, it's really hard to find places like AMS. The Semester School network has similar offerings, but they only last for one semester. But if adolescents wait just a few more years, there's the realm of gap years—all-in-one programs for the age 17 and up crowd.

Dev Carey, that same friend who co-created the Adventure Semester with me, runs an eight-month gap year program with his wife Marian for ages 17–23 on their property, the High Desert Center (HDC). Similar to the Arthur Morgan School, the HDC gap year combines building, backpacking, farming, and road tripping with cooking, cleaning, and consensus decision-making. Sometimes they learn partner dancing, and sometimes they spend long chunks of time in Mexico and Guatemala. In the winter they send participants away to find their own job, internship, or adventure. Dev and Marian are both former teachers, but they don't do any formal academics on their program. Instead, they teach how to butcher a chicken, safely operate a skill saw, and make sense of Colorado River issues in the west. They facilitate multi-hour conversations around big questions like: What does it mean to live in community? How do you motivate yourself to do hard work if you don't have a boss breathing down your neck? How can you fulfill basic needs in life with less than $15,000 a year?

Carl Rogers, the famous psychotherapist, proposed that young people will always learn best from "direct experiential confrontation with practical problems, social problems, ethical and philosophical problems, personal issues, and research problems." I think this is why all-in-one programs like the Arthur Morgan School and High Desert Center hold such great potential to change lives. They directly confront the relevant and engaging issues faced by adolescents and young adults. If you can find and afford such a program, seize the opportunity.

Finally, remember that programs like these frequently offer scholarships and sliding-scale tuitions. Don't let a big price tag automatically turn you away. If your kid might be a great fit for a program that doesn't advertise financial aid, try sending a nicely worded email directly to the office; it might perform wonders.

Notes

For practical resources related to this chapter—and every other chapter in the book—please visit the book's dedicated webpage: https://blakeboles.com/y/

<u>To Play Forever and Ever</u>

I composed Peter Gray's background from his book *Free to Learn* (2013), his chapter in *Evolutionary Perspectives on Child Development and Education* (2016), and personal communications.

<u>To Work Forever and Ever</u>

For extensive details about the lives of children and adolescents in (the many different types of) forager societies, see David Lancy's *The Anthropology of Childhood* (2013).

For more evidence regarding the idea that whenever children were capable of working in earlier societies, they did work, see "Little People" by Joan Acocella (August 10, 2003). https://www.newyorker.com/magazine/2003/08/18/little-people

<u>Worthless Kids</u>

On kids being rendered functionally worthless in the modern economy, see *The End of American Childhood* (2017) by Paula Fass and *Anxious Parents* (2003) by Peter Stearns.

On long-term changes in agricultural employment, see the Employment section of the Wikipedia page "Agriculture in the United States" (undated, accessed November 29, 2019) https://en.wikipedia.org/wiki/Agriculture_in_the_United_States#Employment. Also see "Employment in Agriculture" by Max Roser (undated, accessed November 29, 2019) https://ourworldindata.org/employment-in-agriculture

Gray's quote is from his chapter in the academic book, *Evolutionary Perspectives on Child Development and Education* (2016) edited by David C. Geary and Daniel B. Berch.

The Work of Gaming

The definition of a game, the golf example, the Bernard Suits quote, and all of Jane McGonigal's quotes are from her book, *Reality is Broken* (2010).

It appears that the term "hard fun" originated with Seymour Papert, author of the timeless book, Mindstorms (1980). See "A Tribute to Seymour Papert" by MIT Press (August 3, 2016). https://mitpress.mit.edu/blog/tribute-seymour-papert. Also see "Hard Fun" by Seymour Papert (2002). http://www.papert.org/articles/HardFun.html

Keith Stuart's quote is from "Fortnite Is so Much More Than a Game" (August 17, 2018). https://medium.com/s/greatescape/fortnite-is-so-much-more-than-a-game-3ca829f389f4

For parents with kids who are truly, passionately involved with gaming (in the 40 or more hours-a-week sense), Penelope Trunk offers some helpful insight: "Commitment is essential for doing something that matters" (February 15, 2018). http://blog.penelopetrunk.com/2018/02/15/commitment-is-essential-for-doing-something-that-matters/. Also see "Video games provide a genuine happiness that we find very few other ways" (March 30, 2015). http://education.penelopetrunk.com/2015/03/30/video-games-provide-a-genuine-happiness-that-we-find-very-few-other-ways/

The Magic of Intrinsic Motivation

For more on self-determination theory, see the website of the Center for Self-Determination Theory (https://selfdeterminationtheory.org/) and the 1995 book *Why We Do What We Do* by Edward L. Deci and Richard Flaste.

How to Engage a Teenager

Browse all the Adventure Semester challenges—and watch some high-quality (and hilarious) videos—here: https://blakeboles.com/adventuresemester

Marc Gallivan's quote is from "Give Kids Real Jobs" (June 25, 2018). https://www.alpinevalleyschool.com/blog/2018/6/25/give-kids-real-jobs

The Carl Rogers quote is drawn from Will Richardson's blog post, "On Learning and Common Sense" (October 11, 2017). https://willrichardson.com/on-learning-and-common-sense/

4: YOU HAVE LESS CONTROL THAN YOU THINK

Welcome to the Minefield

How To Be A Mom in 2017: Make sure your children's academic, emotional, psychological, mental, spiritual, physical, nutritional, and social needs are met while being careful not to overstimulate, understimulate, improperly medicate, helicopter, or neglect them in a screen-free, processed foods-free, GMO-free, negative energy-free, plastic-free, body positive, socially conscious, egalitarian but also authoritative, nurturing but fostering of independence, gentle but not overly permissive, pesticide-free two-story, multilingual home preferably in a cul-de-sac with a backyard and 1.5 siblings spaced at least two year[s] apart for proper development also don't forget the coconut oil.

How To Be A Mom In Literally Every Generation Before Ours: Feed them sometimes.

- Bunmi Latidan

When the 29-year-old novelist Kim Brooks first became pregnant, she held two firm convictions about parenting: "I knew it was important, and I knew that I wanted to get it right."

The best way to guard against failure, she assumed, was to do her homework. She dove into the literature on the emotional, social, physical, psychological, and nutritional needs of babies and children, a process not unlike choosing a college major but with actual human lives at stake.

Brooks developed nuanced opinions about "breast-feeding, breast pumps, midwifery, baby-wearing, tummy time, screen time, infant massage, playgroups, hand sanitizer, private versus public school, self-weaning, sleep training, day care, toddler enrichment, and child safety." And while this research helped her feel confident that she was doing her best for her kid, it also left her feeling increasingly self-conscious, uncertain, and overwhelmed. The more she learned about parenting, the less she felt she understood herself and her children.

A turning point came on a spring day in 2011, when Brooks allowed her 4-year-old son to wait in the car while she ran into a store to buy him headphones so he could use his iPad on a flight they were about to take. It was a mild, 50-degree day. Brooks locked the car, child-locked the doors, left the windows cracked open, and returned in five minutes. Unbeknownst to her, a bystander had filmed the entire incident and sent it to the police, who tracked the license plate number. Nine months later, her cell phone rang, and a police officer asked Brooks if she was aware that there was warrant out for her arrest.

In the legal troubles that followed, Brooks reached out to Lenore Skenazy, the prominent spokesperson for free-range parenting who had gained international notoriety as the "world's worst mom" for letting her 9-year-old ride the New York City subway alone. Brooks started telling her story when Skenazy interrupted and offered to finish the story for her:

OK, so, you were running errands with your kid when you decided to leave her in the car for a couple minutes while you ran into a store. The surrounding conditions were perfectly safe, mild weather and such, but when you came out, you found yourself blocked in by a cop car, being yelled at by a nosy, angry onlooker, being accused of child neglect or endangering your child. Is that about right?

Brooks' story wasn't unique after all. It was all too common.

A juvenile court eventually charged Brooks with 100 hours of community service and mandatory parenting education. Brooks didn't actually mind the charges, but she did mind how her son now feared that the police would take him away if he was left alone for only a moment.

Her son's fear mirrored something else that Skenazy had said to her in their conversation:

There's been this huge cultural shift. We now live in a society where most people believe a child cannot be out of your sight for one second, where people think children need constant, total adult supervision. This shift is not rooted in fact. It's not rooted in any true change. It's imaginary. It's rooted in irrational fear.

Brooks began to realize that the kind of parenting that she had been practicing—the normal, modern strain of seemingly research-backed child-rearing—was a factor in this cultural shift. In her quest to become a responsible mother, she had unwittingly contributed to the same culture that prompted a stranger to report her to the police.

What is this culture? Where did it come from? How

grounded is it in reality? And how does it influence your decisions about trusting children, letting them take risks, and sending them to school?[22]

Parenting in the Twenty-First Century

Sometime around 1958, the word "parent" first entered the Merriam-Webster dictionary. Not "parent" as a noun, but "parent" as a verb—a verb that takes an object. Parenting was transforming from an identity to an action. This was a curious shift in language, as the psychologist Alison Gopnick observed, because "to be a wife is not to engage in 'wifing,' to be a friend is not to 'friend'. . .and we don't 'child' our mothers and fathers. Yet these relationships are central to who we are."

This linguistic transformation was just one of the dramatic changes in child-rearing that took place over the past half-decade. Middlebury professor Margaret Nelson neatly described the heart of these changes in her 2010 book, *Parenting Out of Control*:

---

22 A few years ago, I told my friend Tessa, a young adult who had previously joined a few of my adventure programs, that I was writing about parenting. She laughed. "Blake, you don't have kids. Why would anyone listen to you about parenting?" Fair question, Tessa—and perhaps one that passed through your head too, dear reader. Here's the best answer I can offer. Despite the fact that I'm not yet a dad, I have served as a sort of temporary "crazy uncle" to hundreds of teenagers since 2003 through my work at camps and travel programs. This, I believe, has granted me a detached, birds-eye view of youth that lets me make general observations in a way that parents may struggle to do, considering the natural bias toward one's own children. John Holt, the father of unschooling, didn't have any kids himself, but he spent enough time around kids and listened to enough parents to give him an informed opinion on parenting. I'm no John Holt, but I do aspire to follow a similar path—at least until I have a kid of my own.

> When I was raising my children in the 1970s, there were no baby monitors to help me hear them cry in the middle of the night, no cell phones to assist me in keeping track of their whereabouts at every moment, and no expectation that I would know any more about their educational success than they, or a quarterly report card, would tell me. Indeed, although I thought of myself as a relatively anxious parent, I trusted a girl in the third grade to accompany my five-year-old son to and from school, and when he was in first grade, I allowed him to walk that mile by himself...In retrospect, and from the vantage point of watching my younger friends and colleagues with their children today, my parenting style seems, if not neglectful, certainly a mite casual.

When Nelson was raising her children in the 1970s, parenting had begun its transformation into a full-blown industry and a highly technical field dominated by scientific experts. The central idea of this field was that "parents can learn special techniques that will make their children turn out better," as Gopnik puts it. In the '80s and '90s, parenting matured again, much like your kid's favorite Pokémon, into its contemporary, fire-breathing version: something called *intensive parenting*.

Intensive parenting is a tricky thing to define. Sociologist Sharon Hays describes it as any parenting approach that is "child-centered, expert-guided, emotionally absorbing, labor intensive, and financially expensive." Another sociologist, Annette Lareau, considers it a form of "concerted cultivation" in which "parents spend much more time talking to children, answering questions with questions, and treating each child's thought as a special contribution."

But it was Alison Gopnick, again, who found the perfect analogy in her book *The Gardener and the Carpenter*. Modern parenting is goal-oriented parenting, Gopnick observes, much like carpentry is goal-oriented. A gardener, on the other hand, tends to her crops with the hope that they will grow strong, but also knowing that specific outcomes are outside her control.

Goal-oriented attitudes are certainly appropriate for some areas of life. Gopnick concedes that "[working] to achieve a particular outcome is a good model for many crucial human enterprises. It's the right model for carpenters or writers or businessmen. You can judge whether you are a good carpenter or writer or CEO by the quality of your chairs, your books or your bottom line." But when we approach parenting in goal-oriented terms, she warns, we end up thinking of kids as lumps of clay who we might perfectly shape with enough effort and expertise. Just as a master carpenter aspires to build a perfect chair, the intensive parent believes she can "produce the right kind of child, who in turn will become the right kind of adult."

Today, Amazon lists over 80,000 titles in its Parenting books section, and people of all social classes believe in the intensive parenting approach. It is the new normal. How did we arrive at this moment in history? What caused this monumental shift in our attitudes toward parenting?

Plummeting child mortality rates in the late nineteenth century and the rise of effective birth control in the twentieth century led parents to have fewer children and shower more love and attention on each one. Rising prosperity, prohibition of child labor, and the slow shift toward knowledge work nudged children away from their historic role as family breadwinners. As David Lancy observed in *The Anthropology of Childhood*, the parents of developed nations stopped looking at their kids as chattel (economic assets) or changelings (unwanted and inconvenient creatures), and started seeing them as cherubs: innocent, precious, and highly vulnerable individuals.

By the middle of the twentieth century, adults had become more aware of the various physical and emotional threats to young people, and children had gained significant legal protections. Kids were physically safer than ever before in history. Yet a multitude of historical influences conspired to drive parental anxiety. The 1980s brought a few high-profile abduction and child assault cases that were widely broadcasted, seeding the twenty-first century belief in safety at any cost. A stagnation of middle-class wages beginning in the 1970s drove parents to value conventional economic success.[23] Research on brain plasticity in the 1990s prompted parents to provide "highly stimulating" environments—an unwinnable and anxiety-provoking goal if there ever was one, as *The New Yorker* reported in 2008:

> [Brain plasticity] research said that, while the infant brain is, in part, the product of genes, that endowment is just the clay; after birth, it is "sculpted" by the child's experience, the amount of stimulation he receives, above

---

23 As *The New York Times* reported in 2018, "For the first time, it's as likely as not that American children will be less prosperous than their parents. For parents, giving children the best start in life has come to mean doing everything they can to ensure that their children can climb to a higher class, or at least not fall out of the one they were born into."

all in the first three years of life. That finding prompted many programs aimed at stimulating babies whose mothers, for whatever reason (often poverty), seemed likely to neglect them. Social workers drove off to homes deemed at risk, to play with the new baby. But upper-middle-class parents—and marketers interested in them—also read about the brain-plasticity findings, and figured that, if some stimulation is good, more is better. (Hence Baby Einstein.) Later research has provided no support for this. The conclusion, in general, is that the average baby's environment provides all the stimuli he or she needs.

Finally, a simple demographic shift in the twentieth century may explain much of the intensive parenting phenomenon. Since the beginning of time, most families have been large, and most parents have been young. Siblings looked after each other as a matter of necessity. As women began delaying childbirth to seize educational and professional opportunities in the twentieth century, family sizes shrank radically—from approximately seven children in 1850 to two children today. Parents became wealthier and professional childcare became commonplace. The end result was that, from the 1970s onward, children were much more likely to be raised in small families, with fewer siblings but lots of professional adult caretakers.

Fast forward a few decades, and those children are now the adults who are starting families. Because they came from small families that could afford childcare, these parents have virtually no experience in caring for children (i.e., siblings), but they have lots of experience with school and jobs, which is what they've spent most of their lives doing. Therefore, it's natural for this generation of parents to conceive of child-rearing as another goal to be tackled with the same ferocity as their first professional appointment. The internal dialogue, as Alison Gopnick puts it, goes something like this: "If I can just find the right manual or the right secret handbook, I'm going to succeed at this task the same way that I succeeded in my classes or I succeeded at my job." If you've spent your whole life studying intensively and working intensively, then it only makes sense to parent intensively.

The end result of these broad historical and cultural shifts is what the sociologist Frank Furedi calls *parental determinism*: the belief that parents hold almost God-like powers to shape their children's destinies. And with immense powers, of course, comes immense responsibilities. According to the dogma of intensive parenting, if your kid fails, then it's your fault—and if your kid succeeds, it's to your credit. Either way, the stakes are high, which means you can't afford to mess around—especially with any wacky "alternatives." Get your kid into the best possible school, micromanage them to ensure top performance, and make sure they don't deviate from the prescribed path to success, no matter the cost.

Meet Judith Rich Harris

Intensive parenting is so pervasive today that it can be hard to see. Yet we must see it, and name it, because of the harm it can cause to children, parent-child relationships, and our culture at large (as evidenced by Kim Brooks' experience leaving her kid alone for five minutes).

I see two broad ways of combating the tide of intensive parenting. The first approach is to adopt a radically different view of parenting, join online groups filled with fellow true believers, and surround your children with families who share your exact philosophy. This may make life easy, because you don't have to spend much time convincing non-believers, but it's also essentially the approach of a separatist movement.

The second approach involves holding a radically different view of parenting while also making a conscious choice to remain part of mainstream society. This path is less comfortable. You'll find yourself swimming in the ever-rising waters of intensive parenting, needing to defend your unconventional choices. Yet if you're determined to give your child more of the world, not less, then I believe that the second path is the one to take. And if there's one thing that makes the second path easier, it's intellectual ammunition—which is why I'd like you to meet Judith Rich Harris.

In 1960, Harris was working on her Ph.D. in psychology at Harvard when she was unexpectedly kicked out of the program due to her purported lack of "originality and independence." Leaving Harvard with only a master's degree, she married one of her fellow graduate students and had two daughters. Chronic health issues prompted her to seek home-based work, so she became a writer of introductory college psychology textbooks.

While poring over the scientific literature for her textbooks, Harris started noticing errors—big, significant errors—in the research behind child development. This prompted her to begin her own line of research, bringing together disparate psychological studies in a brand-new way. She shared her findings in an article for *Psychological Review*—the field's most distinguished academic journal—

that earned her instant acclaim, despite her lack of a Ph.D. or university affiliation.[24] Harris capitalized on the moment by writing The Nurture Assumption that expanded on her research, catapulted her into the national spotlight, and led to her nomination of a Pulitzer Prize.

So what was Harris' big message? What did she have to say about children that captured the world's attention?

In a nutshell, Harris told parents to stop parenting. "The idea that we can make our children turn out any way we want is an illusion," she wrote. Children's destinies are written by forces largely outside of anyone's control. While you can (and should) develop a strong, loving relationship with your child, Harris told parents, you shouldn't try to "parent" in the goal-oriented sense, because it's both futile and damaging.

Harris published her book in the late nineties, just as intensive parenting was coming of age, so it's easy to see why it struck a nerve. Harris essentially threw a big, wet blanket over the idea that parents can precisely control how their children turn out in the long run. The "grandmother from New Jersey" (as some critics called her) crashed the intensive parenting party and told everyone to go home.

Twenty years later, most people still don't like Harris' message. Even within alternative education circles, her ideas aren't popular. This is partly due to long-standing misinterpretations of her research—such as the idea that "parents don't matter"—and partly due to its ego-bruising nature.

---

24 The article was so influential that the American Psychological Association awarded her the prized George A. Miller Award for an "outstanding recent article in psychology," named after the very same man who kicked her out of Harvard 37 years earlier.

No one likes to be told that they are unimportant, and our culture has consistently told parents that they have the most important job in the world. Despite all this, I believe her message is vitally important and empowering, because it tells you to enjoy your children for who they are, to support whatever educational path seems to fit them best, and ultimately, to relax.

The Nurture Assumption

If you enjoy geeking out on social science, then you'll enjoy this next section, in which I summarize Harris' arguments in order to help you duel with the true believers of intensive parenting. But if you don't, allow me to cut right to the punchline.

In *The Nurture Assumption*, Judith Rich Harris says that two major factors influence how kids turn out in the long run: genes (nature) and the environment (nurture). Genes are out of our control, and we tend to grossly underestimate their influence. Environment includes many factors, of which parents are assumed to be the most important. But according to Harris' research, kids actually take far more cues from their peers. Parents do shape their kids within the context of the household, but that's as far as their power goes. When it comes to long-run personality traits and life outcomes, your kid's fate is overwhelmingly determined by the genes you've already given them and the peer groups that surround them—which is what makes intensive parenting futile at best and harmful at worst.

So what can you do as a parent? You can help your kid connect to positive peer groups instead of negative ones, and you can focus on building a strong one-on-one relationship with your kid. If you never pick up *The Nurture Assumption*, I hope you'll read this quote twice, because it strikes at the heart of the matter:

> People sometimes ask me, "So you mean it doesn't matter how I treat my child?" They never ask, "So you mean it doesn't matter how I treat my husband?" or "So you mean it doesn't matter how I treat my wife?" And yet the situation is similar. I don't expect that the way I act toward my husband today is going to determine what kind of person he will be tomorrow. I do expect, however, that it will affect how happy he is to live with me and whether we will remain good friends.

We want our kids to grow up happy. We want to remain life-long friends with them. Controlling, coercing, and actively molding children will not achieve that end. Harris implores us to be humble, to acknowledge how little power we have over our children, and to love them for who they are.

Finally, an important question: is Judith Rich Harris just a rogue scholar who no one takes seriously? While the first edition (1998) and second edition (2009) were indeed attacked by mainstream critics and nit-picked by fellow scientists, it appears that no one has yet mounted a serious challenge to her ideas. When she passed away in 2018, Harvard psychologist Steven Pinker described her findings as "abundantly replicated," and other mainstream scientists have cited and defended her work in recent years. So yes, she deserves to be taken seriously.

That's the short story. Now, on to the juicy details.

*   *   *

It's easy to assume that parents strongly influence their kids, as Harris writes in the beginning of *The Nurture Assumption*:

How can I question something for which there is so much evidence? You can see it with your own eyes: parents do have effects on their kids. The child who has been beaten looks cowed in the presence of her parents. The child whose parents have been wimpy runs rampant over them. The child whose parents failed to teach morality behaves immorally. The child whose parents don't think he will accomplish much doesn't accomplish much. . .Parents who care for their babies in a loving, responsive way tend to have babies who are securely attached to them and who develop into self-confident, friendly children. Parents who talk to their children, listen to them, and read to them tend to have bright children who do well in school. Parents who provide firm—but not rigid—limits for their children have children who are less likely to get into trouble. Parents who treat their children harshly tend to have children who are aggressive or anxious, or both. Parents who behave in an honest, kind, and conscientious manner with their children are likely to have children who also behave in an honest, kind, and conscientious manner.

As a psychology textbook author, Harris knew that there was a tremendous amount of research backing these standard findings. But as she dove into the research, Harris began to suspect that psychologists weren't connecting the dots in the right way.

Language was one of the first clues. While at Harvard, Harris lived above a Russian couple who spoke with distinct Russian accents—but whose children spoke perfect English, even with the same Boston/Cambridge accent as the local kids. "It puzzled me," Harris wrote. "Obviously, babies don't learn to speak on their own; obviously, they learn their language from their parents. . .[but] even the five-year-old was a more competent speaker of English than her mother." Then she read about upper-class British boys who typically spent little time with their fathers: their first decade was with nannies and siblings, and their second decade happened at elite boarding schools. Yet upon returning from boarding school, these boys possessed the same upper-class accents and demeanors as their fathers.

If children learned language and culture without their parents' help, Harris started to wonder, what else might they be learning on their own? Could this "learning" include personality traits? If a pleasant and competent child turned into a pleasant and competent adult, was it necessarily because of their parents? Was it causation or correlation?

What if, Harris mused, we treat our children the way we do because of who they *already are*:

> [As] most parents realize shortly after the birth of their second child, children come into this world already different from each other. Their parents treat them differently because of their different characteristics. A fearful child is reassured; a bold one is cautioned. A smiley baby is kissed and played with; an unresponsive one is fed, diapered, and put in its crib. The effects the socialization researchers are interested in are parent-to-child effects: the parent has an

effect on the child. There are also effects that go in the opposite direction: the child has an effect on the parent. . .[Children] who are hugged are more likely to be nice, children who are spanked are more likely to be unpleasant. Turn that statement around and you get one that is equally plausible: nice children are more likely to be hugged, unpleasant children are more likely to be spanked. Do the hugs cause the children's niceness, or is the children's niceness the reason why they are hugged, or are both true? Do spankings make children unpleasant, or are parents more likely to lose their temper with unpleasant children, or are both true?

Taller parents produce taller children. Parents with certain illnesses pass those illnesses down to their children. And the same is true with personality traits. Timid parents are more likely to produce timid children and aggressive parents are more likely to produce aggressive children. Harris argued that while this is scientifically valid, it's also tricky to prove because parents and children are both biological relatives *and* housemates. Parents provide their children with both genes and environment, making it hard to figure which is responsible for shaping a child.

Enter twin studies. If you observe identical twins (i.e., those who share identical genes) who are separated at birth and raised by different families, you can isolate the effects of parenting. And if parenting does, in fact, make a big difference, then identical twins reared apart should turn out to be much different people.

Many such studies have been conducted, and the results are shocking. The 2018 documentary *Three Identical Strangers* offers one glimpse into such a study. Three identical siblings (triplet boys) were separated at birth and raised by three different families. When they reunited at age 19, they discovered that all three of them danced the same, preferred the same brand of cigarettes, were attracted to the same type of women, and wrestled in high school. Later, as they aged, all three struggled with mental health issues. Despite the fact that the boys were raised with radically different parenting styles (and in homes with different income levels), they turned out more or less the same.

A 1995 piece in *The New Yorker* highlighted similarly mind-boggling studies, such as when twin boys raised apart in Germany and Trinidad were reunited, "both wearing rectangular wire-frame glasses, short mustaches, and blue two-pocket shirts with epaulets; both were in the habit of reading magazines back to front and flushing toilets before using them; both liked to startle people by sneezing in elevators."

Harris cites such fascinating stories in her book, as well as less colorful but more consequential large-scale twin studies (such as the Minnesota Twin Family Study, which continues to this day). These studies have proven beyond any reasonable doubt that genetics have a major influence on children's personality traits, accounting for roughly fifty percent of measurable variability.[25]

All parents accept that genetics plays *some* role in how their kids turn out, of course, even if they have trouble swal-

---

25 Genetic variation, heritability, and gene-environment interactions are fascinating and very, very complicated. See Robert Sapolsky's 2018 book, *Behave,* for an accessible discussion of these topics.

lowing the words "fifty percent." But the home environment must still play an important role, right?

Enter adoption studies. If two genetically unrelated siblings share the same parents and home environment, then they should turn out similarly, right? Yet Harris shows how adopted siblings share precious few personality traits. As a 2011 academic review summarized it, "For most psychological characteristics, correlations for adoptive 'siblings' hover near zero."

Harris concludes that we give the home environment far more credit than it's due. If a kid's parents "work or don't work, read or don't read, drink or don't drink, fight or don't fight, stay married or don't stay married," they'll probably turn out similarly in the end. If the home is "an apartment or a farmhouse, spacious or crowded, messy or tidy, full of art supplies and tofu or full of auto parts and Twinkies," they'll probably end up the same.

Raised in daycare? Doesn't matter. Raised by a same-sex couple? Doesn't matter. Only child? Doesn't matter. In the long run, all these supposedly important factors in a child's life simply didn't have any measurable effects on kids' personalities or major life outcomes, Harris showed.

Are you starting to see why her book garnered national controversy?

By bringing together a number of noncontroversial psychology findings in a brand new way, Harris threw a wrench into conventional thinking about child-rearing, one that the scientific community still doesn't know how to handle: the idea that kids' destinies are far less shaped by parenting styles, home environments, and lifestyles than we like to believe.

Do parents matter? On first glance, it seems like Harris is saying "not at all." That's the popular misconception of her work, and it's far from the truth. For starters, Harris made it clear that she only paid attention to studies that fell within the normal spectrum of responsible parenting. She heartily acknowledged that child abuse, trauma, and neglect were real threats that damaged children—and parents have an obligation to treat their kids with basic dignity and respect.

Parents also mattered in another very large way, according to Harris, based on how they influenced their child's peer groups. This brings us to the heart of her work, which takes a bit more explaining.

*   *   *

Consider, again, the magic of language acquisition. Virtually every child in the world learns to speak their native tongue, including orphans and those living in dire poverty. The children of first-generation immigrants learn new languages with shocking speed, even when their parents don't speak a word of it at home. Deaf children become rapidly proficient in signing when their parents have no idea how to sign themselves. Yet no child is born knowing a language. They acquire it through their environment, which consists of countless factors, including parents, teachers, peers, television, physical environmental factors (like nutritious food and clean air), random events, and so on. Because children spend so much time around their parents, we easily assume that much of the environmental influence comes from parents. Harris' radical idea was this: most effects that parents appear to have on kids can actually be chalked up to genetics and peers.

How do immigrant children learn new languages? From their peers in their neighborhoods and in schools. How do deaf children learn to sign? From their peers at a school for the deaf. How did children in early societies learn to speak fluently without formal schooling? By hanging around their peers in mixed-age groups.

Language is an easy way to see how important peers might be to child development. But what about bigger things, like personality traits? Beyond synthesizing the research of others, Judith Rich Harris made an original contribution to psychology by coining something she called "group social-ization theory": the idea that children and adults live in two fundamentally different worlds—and children's ultimate loy-alties will always belong to their peers.

Harris observes how kids don't like mixing the worlds of home (parents) and school (peers). They are often so desper-ate to fit in with their peer groups that they'll avoid telling their friends about troubles at home, just as they hide school-yard bullying from their parents. Harris herself "was a social outcast for four years of [her] childhood," during which her classmates wouldn't talk to her—yet her parents never found out.

Harris further notes how kids are especially prone to thinking in terms "us versus them" and forming groups based on shared traits. Children typically associate with those unlike themselves only out of necessity, for example, when a social group is very small. Once the social group becomes big enough, children tend to automatically divide themselves into same-age, same-sex, and same-interest subgroups—much to the chagrin of diversity-minded parents.

Because humans are so group-oriented, Harris proposes, children will always value, imitate, and learn from their peers before their parents. "Kids versus adults" is one of the earliest distinctions that humans make, and it's a powerful one. Adolescents don't rebel because they want to be more adult-like; they rebel because they want to differentiate themselves from adults. Malcolm Gladwell's 1998 *New Yorker* article about *The Nurture Assumption* even references Peter Gray's support of Harris' group socialization theory:

If developmental psychology were an enterprise conducted by children, there is no question that peer relationships would be at the top of the list. . .[J]ust look at them. Whom do they want to please? Are they wearing the kind of clothing that other kids are wearing or the kind that their parents are wearing? If the other kids are speaking another way, whose language are they going to learn? And, from an evolutionary perspective, whom should they be paying attention to? Their parents—the members of the previous generation—or their peers, who will be their future mates and future collaborators? It would [be] more adaptive for them to be better attuned to the nuances of their peers' behavior. That just makes a lot of sense.

So, what, in the end, are parents good for? A message that Harris emphasized over and over in her book was this: your personal relationship with your child is certainly important, but it's no more important than a relationship with a spouse, sibling, friend, lover, or parent. In a romantic relationship, for example, you want to feel unconditionally loved, and you want your daily life to be enriched by your partner.

In these regards, a relationship with a child is no different.

Harris makes a helpful analogy to marriage, explaining how your spouse will change how you act over time but won't fundamentally change your personality:

> You can learn things from the person you're married to. Marriage can change your opinions and influence your choice of a career or a religion. But it doesn't change your personality, except in temporary, context-dependent ways.

When it comes to children, Harris showed that parents do, in fact, influence their kid's religious beliefs, political beliefs, musical talents, and career plans. Yet all of these are fairly superficial in the larger scheme of things, because they don't force the child to choose between parents and peers:

> Some things just don't come up in the context of the peer group. This is true nowadays of religion. Unless they attend a religious school, practicing a religion is something children don't do with their peers: they do it with their parents. That is why parents still have some power to give their kids their religion. Parents have some power to impart any aspect of their culture that involves things done in the home; cooking is a good example. Anything learned at home and kept at home—not scrutinized by the peer group— may be passed on from parents to their kids.

Imagine if a good friend of yours moved into your house for 15 years, and you spent most mornings, evenings, and weekends with her. Clearly, her career ambitions, musical talents, politics, and favorite recipes might rub off on you (and vice versa). But would you expect this friend to change into a fundamentally more ambitious, reserved, or conscientious person? If she did, would you chalk it up to your direct influence, or would you just as quickly attribute such changes to her co-workers, other friends, or perhaps even her favorite television shows?

Now imagine if that same friend was trying to shape, control, or change *you* in some big ways—if she was attempting to make you more relaxed or assertive or ambitious. How long before you would show that friend the door?

Your home is just an 18-year-long stop on your child's journey through life. They will adapt to the rules of your house in order to make their time there as enjoyable as possible, but as soon as they leave home and enter the world of their peers—whether that means going to school for the day or moving out entirely—they will cast off their adaptations "as easily as the dorky sweater their mother made them wear," Harris jokes. A troublemaker at home may be an angel in school, and vice versa.

The true power of a parent, Harris suggests, lies in the ability to form a warm, caring, long-term, one-on-one relationship with a child—and to not abuse that power:

> You have little power to determine how your children will behave when they're not with you, but you have a great deal of power to determine how they will behave at home. You have little power to determine how the world will treat them, but you have a great deal of power to determine how happy or unhappy they will be at home.

Parents *matter*, as the psychologist and geneticist Robert Plomin likes to say—they just don't make a *difference*. Yes, it matters how you treat your kid, in the same way that it matters how you treat your friends, siblings, business partners, or spouse. These are all important relationships that determine the quality of our lives. The difference is that kids are younger, smaller, economically dependent, and legally prohibited from working, signing contracts, owning property, and otherwise leading their own lives. (Because of the vulnerability inherent in these differences, it's a moral imperative for a parent—even more than a spouse or business partner—to engage with kindness and care.)

Like a good friend or supportive spouse, you can still hold your kid to a reasonable standard of behavior. You can still insist that they have manners. You can still be frank and direct with them. But you don't have to worry about constantly entertaining them or monitoring their emotions. "Parents are meant to enjoy parenting," Harris reminds us. "If you are not enjoying it, maybe you're working too hard."[26]

Tom Hodgkinson, author of the funny and insightful book, *The Idle Parent*, makes the same point in another way:

There is nothing so corrosive or pestilent as resentment stewing in the breast. Imagine making all those sacrifices,

---

26 Relinquishing a sense of control doesn't mean relinquishing all authority. Harris channels the voice of radical educator A.S. Neill–whose catchphrase was "freedom, not license"–when she writes, "[Parents] are meant to be in charge. But nowadays they are so hesitant about exerting their authority–a hesitancy imposed upon them by the advice-givers–that it is difficult for them to run the home in an effective manner. . . The experiences of previous generations show that it is possible to rear well-adjusted children without making them feel that they are the center of the universe or that a time-out is the worst thing that could happen to them if they disobey. Parents know better than their children and should not feel diffident about telling them what to do. Parents, too, have a right to a happy and peaceful home life."

putting yourself out for your children, going without—and then they turn round and go junkie on you in some kind of Amy Winehouse / Pete Doherty nightmare. No, there is no room for martyrs in the world of the idle parent. Our happiness comes first. And that is the right way round; as a cab driver said to me the other day of his kids: "They're happy because we're happy." Do not suffer. Enjoy your life.

Express your needs without abusing your power. Don't let anyone run roughshod over you. Be neither a servant nor a tyrant. This is the same advice that will make you a good sibling, friend, housemate, co-worker, spouse—and parent, too.

At the end of the day, Judith Rich Harris wants to free you from the fear, guilt, and anxiety of intensive parenting:

You've followed their advice and where has it got you? They've made you feel guilty if you don't love all your children equally, though it's not your fault if nature made some kids more lovable than others. They've made you feel guilty if you don't give them enough quality time, though your kids seem to prefer to spend their quality time with their friends. . .Worst of all, they've made you feel guilty if anything goes wrong with your child. It's easy to blame parents for everything: they're sitting ducks. Fair game ever since Freud lit his first cigar.

God, I love this woman.

Picking Peers

You now possess some intellectual ammunition for resisting the onslaught of intensive parenting. When a helpful busy-body insists that you should adopt a certain parenting style, instructional method, or new-fangled toy that will radically change your kid's life, you can smile, breathe, thank them for their suggestion—and gracefully ignore it. Thank you, Judith Rich Harris.

But Harris' message does add one big item to a parent's to-do list: ensuring that your kid is surrounded by excellent peers. Because as Harris' group socialization theory made abundantly clear, peers are the ones who dramatically shape your child, and that means that you do have the power—at least for a little while—to shape your kid via their peer group.

Here's an example from my own life. When I was 11, my dad asked me if I wanted to go to a two-week wilderness summer camp in California that he'd discovered, Deer Crossing Camp (the same camp where I led the Ascent trips). I said yes, and come July, he waved me goodbye as I boarded a charter bus to the California High Sierra.

I didn't know it at that moment, but this was a very different kind of summer camp: one that celebrated positive thinking and can-do attitudes. The first thing I learned at Deer Crossing was that campers were not allowed to bring their *T'naci* monsters into camp. What the heck is a *T'naci* monster, I thought. Answer: it's the phrase "I can't" spelled backwards. This was the camp director's clever way of ensuring that kids wouldn't utter those two little words—and therefore limit their possible achievements—at his high-challenge wilderness summer camp.

At first I didn't think that anyone would really uphold this language ban; it was probably just some cheesy policy that campers mostly ignored. I was wrong. At this camp, virtually no one said "I can't." If I let those two infamous words slip out of my mouth, as I often did in the first few days, the camp staff, the returning campers, and even some of new campers would quickly notice and instruct me to say something else: either *T'naci*, "I choose not to," or "I could if I" (after which you were supposed to insert some constructive reasoning).

After two weeks of fighting my *T'naci* monster, I returned home convinced. I started telling my parents that I no longer wanted to say "I can't." This eventually wore off as I spent time around my school friends, but then I returned to Deer Crossing the next summer and received another dose of *T'naci* culture. I attended for a total of four summers, and by the time I was 15, the Deer Crossing community had genuinely shaped me into a young person who avoided knee-jerk negativity, looked for solutions, and believed in his ability to overcome most obstacles.

Would I have accepted the *T'naci* monster story if it had been my parents—rather than an entire summer camp community—who tried to instill it in me? No way. I would have written off this crazy idea simply because it came from my parents rather than my peers (and some non-parental adults). The same character traits that my parents would have pulled their hair out trying to drill into me at home were instilled, almost effortlessly, through my immersion in the Deer Crossing community.

Peer groups can accomplish much that parents cannot. This means, to the extent that you can determine who your children spend time around, you can indeed shape them. This power dwindles as children grow up and increasingly choose their own friends, but as my time at Deer Crossing shows, positive interventions are always possible.

Sometimes shaping your kid's peer group is as simple as bailing them out of cruel peer environments. Consider a study by the sociologist Anne-Marie Ambert, who asked her students to write about the most upsetting events in their lives. Only nine percent identified something their parents did, while more than a third cited their the actions of their peers. Ambert concluded:

> There is far more negative treatment by peers than by parents. . . In these autobiographies, one reads accounts of students who had been happy and well adjusted, but quite rapidly began deteriorating psychologically, sometimes to the point of becoming physically ill and incompetent in school, after experiences such as being rejected by peers, excluded, talked about, racially discriminated against, laughed at, bullied, sexually harassed, taunted, chased or beaten.

Sometimes, it's simply a part of life to learn how to cope with challenging social situations. Other times—as within many conventional schools—bullying, harassment, discrimination, and exclusion run rampant, leading to toxic levels of stress. This may explain why so many small alternative schools and self-directed learning centers work well for young people: they are overwhelmingly friendly, inclusive, and respectful places. (Home-based educational environments offer excellent respite from traumatic school situations, too. In *The Nurture Assumption*, Harris even gives homeschooling her explicit stamp of approval, "as long as the child isn't completely isolated from peers.")

All those adventures mentioned in the last chapter—the summer camps, wilderness trips, group travel programs, and boarding schools—offer excellent opportunities to immerse your child in a peer group that may shape him for the better. These can be especially powerful for adolescent homeschoolers with limited social opportunities.

Not Back to School Camp, the summer camp for teenage self-directed learners where I've worked for over a dozen years, has done more good for adolescent social lives than any other place I've worked. I've seen unschoolers from rural Nevada, Alaska, and Alabama develop friendships through Not Back to School Camp that become their social lifelines throughout the rest of the year.

Will every such program provide a positive peer group? Of course not. It's always risky to send your kid to any kind of program where strangers will have a chance to influence her. Yet risk is part of the game. To eliminate risk would be tantamount to controlling every single one of your child's peer interactions—and that would be yet another manifestation of intensive parenting.

"Who is speaking up, today, for a young person's right to a private life, to secrets, unshared thoughts, unmonitored conversations and relationships?" the novelist Jess Row asks. Do your best to give your child a positive peer group, but let them have their privacy, too. For me, that was the best part of summer camp: living my own life, developing my own thoughts, and figuring out who I was, separate from my parents. Thanks to the space they gave me, I only appreciated them more when I returned home.

Browsing and Hanging Out, Reconsidered

We now have the tools to understand another phenomenon: why self-directed kids spend so much of their time browsing the internet and hanging out with each other (i.e., socializing).

Browsing and hanging out are the primary activities—along with gaming—that take place in small alternative schools and self-directed learning centers, and they tend to make parents very uncomfortable. Seen through the lens of peer-orientation, however, these things start to make more sense.

Let's start with dreaded YouTube. Why do kids everywhere naturally gravitate toward YouTube as soon as they have a moment of free time? Peter Gray would argue that young people flock there (and to other on-demand video content) for the same reason that they flock to movies, television, magazines, books, or (once upon a time) radio: because they want to understand their culture. They want to learn how the world works, and YouTube is simply the best way to do that today. Or in simpler terms: YouTube is *awesome*. As the blogger Brendan Leonard observes:

> On YouTube, men and women I'll never meet have taught me how to use stoves, execute better kick turns on skis, trim my skins, rewire light switches, remove tile, edit video in Adobe Premiere, and all sorts of other things. It's saved me weeks, maybe months of trying to figure things out, and maybe saved fingers I would have lost in home improvement accidents. Sometimes these people are anonymous, sometimes they have usernames or real names that we forget, and most of the time we never meet them

in person. Maybe they make no money off their YouTube videos, or a few dollars a month or year. Maybe they don't care if they're reimbursed at all—they just want to share knowledge. . .Whatever motivates people to put useful information on YouTube, I am grateful. Yes, 50 years ago, or even 20 years ago, we would have had to learn skills from mentors, or books, and there's a little something lost in not having an in-person relationship. But if I need to know how to install an electrical outlet at 10:30 a.m. on a Sunday, a pixelated video made by a guy from New Jersey who knows what he's doing is pretty damn convenient. As long as you don't get sidetracked clicking on Best Fails Of The Year and lose track of 20 minutes, anyway.

Judith Rich Harris told us that kids desperately want to understand *their* world. YouTube is one good way to do this; social media is another. Want to understand the culture of your global peer group? Just spend an hour on Snapchat, Instagram, Tumblr, Twitter, or Reddit. For all the potential downsides of social media, one thing is clear: they are incredibly powerful enculturation tools.

Prior to the rise of the internet in the 1990s, it might have been possible for homeschooled and alternatively schooled kids to miss out on peer trends; sheltering was truly possible. But today, thanks to our widely available communication technologies, sheltering your kids is bound to fail unless you raise them totally off the grid in a truly cult-like fashion. If you ever let your kids go online, they will be exposed to global youth culture, and if you don't, their peers at school (or their alternative school or homeschool co-op) will fill them in on what they missed.

If browsing is how kids orient themselves to rules of their global peer group, then "hanging out" is how they learn the local rules. For example: How do you become part of a group? How do you make people laugh? How do cliques form? How do you navigate conflicting loyalties? How do you gracefully reject a bid for your attention? How do you maintain a friendship? How do you end a friendship? How do you flirt? How do you make your voice heard in a group? How do you gain respect and natural authority? Tackling these important questions is what's going on under the surface of "hanging out," which is why it's so important for young people to have space—some space, any space—where they can act with true autonomy, free from the meddling of adults.

If your kid decides to unschool or attend a highly alternative school, then yes, they will probably spend lots of time browsing screens and hanging out—especially in the beginning. This is okay. Your kid is learning how their world operates. Let it happen.

Eyes on the Prize

Kim Brooks, the mom who went to court for leaving her four-year-old safely in a car for five minutes, met with free-range parenting advocate Lenore Skenazy a second time in New York City. Discussing her unfortunate odyssey over coffee and bagels, Brooks found herself digging into her own memories of childhood. Brooks' fondest memories of her parents, she realized, didn't arise from any type of goal-oriented parenting:

> [I recall] long walks or bike rides with them down to the lake, family dinners together, and also the moments

when they'd stop hassling me and give me space, let me do something new on my own, like the first time I got to go to the mall without an adult, or the first time I got to spend the night at a friend's house, or, later, go with friends to a movie, or on a date. Later, there was the adventure of going off to college, of traveling abroad on my own for the first time—the thrill of that, of feeling autonomous and alive in the world. . .Many of my most joyful memories involved these moments of sudden independence when the world opened up, when I felt myself alone and awake in it; I knew my parents' love most acutely in these moments of expanding distance, of letting go.

In this chapter I've given you some ammunition to fight back against intensive parenting. According to the parents I've known, this will not be an easy fight. Much like choosing to unschool or sending your kid to a radical alternative school, it's difficult to fight intensive parenting when your friends and neighbors are sticking to the conventional path. It's difficult when other parents don't just have differing opinions, but they judge you, openly and harshly, for doing things that you consider safe and reasonable. And it's difficult to remember that loving one's children and loving the act of parenting are not the same thing.

Opting out of intensive parenting takes courage, but it ends up being more fun and less work, because you stop worrying about things that are truly out of your control. It also lets you move away from the role of boss or manager"of your child's life and into the role of consultant. I'm a big fan of this analogy, which I borrow from William Stixrud and Ned Johnson in *The Self-Driven Child*.

Imagine the role of a talented business consultant:

- She possesses more knowledge and expertise than her client.
- She helps her client identify the right problem, asks the right questions, and sets priorities.
- She asks what her client is willing to commit to, or sacrifice, to reach a specific goal.
- When her client fails to reach a goal, she doesn't lose her wits or become overly emotionally invested, because then she becomes part of the problem.
- She gives honest advice, but she never forces something upon her client.
- She knows that ultimately, it's her client's business at stake, not hers. She is not responsible for the success or failure of that business.

That, more or less, is the recipe for non-intensive parenting.

Ben Hewitt, the unschooling father whose kid ended up choosing conventional school over unschooling, describes the same idea in different words:

I've come to believe that modern parents too often do a poor job of distinguishing between responsibility and control. Which is to say, it is our responsibility to provide a base level of material, intellectual, and emotional support for our children, along with experiences that will enrich their lives. But we cannot control the outcome. Perhaps our children will develop into the capable, compassionate, and successful (however we define success) people we fervently want them to be. And perhaps, in ways that may be disappointing or flat-out painful, they will not.

"Loving children doesn't give them a destination," writes Alison Gopnick, "it gives them sustenance for the journey." Let's help kids chart their own paths, "even if the path they take isn't one we would choose ourselves, or even one we would choose for them."

I believe Judith Rich Harris would agree.

Notes

For practical resources related to this chapter—and every other chapter in the book—please visit the book's dedicated webpage: https://blakeboles.com/y/

<u>Welcome to the Minefield</u>

Bunmi Latidan's quote: https://www.facebook.com/BunmiKLaditan/posts/how-to-be-a-mom-in-2017-make-sure-your-childrens-academic-emotional-psychologica/1899244270322560/

Kim Brooks' story and quotes (including Lenore Skenazy's) are from "The day I left my son in the car" by Kim Brooks (January 1, 2015). https://www.salon.com/2014/12/31/the_day_i_left_my_son_in_the_car_2/ and "The Struggle To Reclaim Parenting" by Kim Brooks (April 21, 2015). https://www.buzzfeednews.com/article/kimbrooks/reclaiming-parenting

<u>Parenting in the Twenty-First Century</u>

The rise of intensive parenting is well-documented in these four articles:

"The Relentlessness of Modern Parenting" by Claire Cain Miller (December 25, 2018). https://www.nytimes.com/2018/12/25/upshot/the-relentlessness-of-modern-parenting.html

"A Manifesto Against 'Parenting'" by Alison Gopnick (July 8, 2016). https://www.wsj.com/articles/a-manifesto-against-parenting-1467991745

"All Joy and No Fun" by Jennifer Senior (July 2, 2010). http://nymag.com/news/features/67024/

"'Intensive' Parenting Is Now the Norm in America" by Joe Pinsker (January 16, 2019). https://www.theatlantic.com/family/archive/2019/01/intensive-helicopter-parenting-inequality/580528/

I calculated the 80,000 parenting titles on Amazon.com in January 2019.

On the emerging perception of children as precious and unique individuals who are highly susceptible to risks, see *Anxious Parents* by Peter Stearns (2003).

On the role of economic anxiety in shifting parenting approaches in the '60s, '70s, and '80s, see "The Child Trap" by Joan Acocella (November 9, 2008). https://www.newyorker.com/magazine/2008/11/17/the-child-trap

The *New York Times* quote ("For the first time…") is from "The Relentlessness of Modern Parenting" by Claire Cain Miller (December 25, 2018). https://www.nytimes.com/2018/12/25/upshot/the-relentlessness-of-modern-parenting.html

On changing family sizes, see "The decline of the large US family, in charts" by Ephrat Livni and Dan Kopf (October 11, 2017). https://qz.com/1099800/average-size-of-a-us-family-from-1850-to-the-present/

On parents treating child-rearing like a job or school assignment, see "What Kind Of Parent Are You: Carpenter Or Gardener?" by Sasha Ingber (May 28, 2018). https://www.npr.org/sections/goatsandsoda/2018/05/28/614386847/what-kind-of-parent-are-you-carpenter-or-gardener

The brain plasticity quote is from "The Child Trap" by Joan Acocella (November 9, 2008). https://www.newyorker.com/magazine/2008/11/17/the-child-trap

Meet Judith Rich Harris

All quotes and references to Harris' research in this section and the next, unless otherwise noted, are from the second edition of *The Nurture Assumption* by Judith Rich Harris (2009).

Harris' backstory is from "Judith Rich Harris, 80, Dies; Author Played Down the Role of Parents" by Katharine Q. Seelye (January 1, 2019). https://www.nytimes.com/2019/01/01/obituaries/judith-rich-harris-dies.html

Malcolm Gladwell's article in *The New Yorker* is "Do Parents Matter?" (August 10, 1998). https://www.newyorker.com/magazine/1998/08/17/do-parents-matter

On Harris' Pulitzer Prize nomination: "She Persisted: Lessons From the Life of Judith Rich Harris" by David Myers (January 10, 2019) https://community.macmillan.com/community/the-psychology-community/blog/2019/01/10/she-persisted-lessons-from-the-life-of-judith-rich-harris

The British psychologist Naomi Fisher, who is also the mother of two young self-directed learners, pointed out to me that middle-class unschooling parents may display the characteristic traits of intensive parents to the extent that their unschooling is a form of "concerted cultivation" (instead of the more detached parenting style I characterize in this book) and to the extent that they embrace "attachment parenting," which itself is a form of intensive parenting.

The Nurture Assumption

Steven Pinker's comment is from "Judith Rich Harris: 1938 - 2018" (January 9, 2019): https://www.edge.org/conversation/judith_rich_harris-judith-rich-harris-1938-2018

Stanford biologist Robert Sapolsky defended the essence of Harris' research in his 2017 book, *Behave*. "As the dust has settled, current opinion tends to be that peer influences are underappreciated, but parents still are plenty important, including by influencing what peer groups their kids experience." Alison Gopnick did the same in *The Gardener and the Carpenter*: "[It] is very difficult to find any reliable, empirical relation between the small variations in what parents do—the variations that are the focus of parenting—and the resulting adult traits of their children. There is very little evidence that conscious decisions about co-sleeping or not, letting your children 'cry it out' or holding them till they fall asleep, or forcing them to do extra homework or letting them play have reliable and predictable long-term effects on who those children become. From an empirical perspective, parenting is a mug's game."

For a few challenges to Harris' assumptions, see "Parenting and the Non-Shared Environment" by William Eden (October 14, 2013). http://becomingeden.com/parenting-and-the-non-shared-environment/

For a summary of *Three Identical Strangers*, see "Separated-at-birth triplets met tragic end after shocking psych experiment" by Sara Stewart (June 23, 2018). https://nypost.com/2018/06/23/these-triplets-were-separated-at-birth-for-a-twisted-psych-study/

On twin studies, see "Double Mystery" by Lawrence Wright (July 31, 1995). https://www.newyorker.com/magazine/1995/08/07/double-mystery

The quote about personality correlations between adoptive siblings is from "Why are children in the same family so different from one another?" by Robert Plomin and Denise Daniels in the *International Journal of Epidemiology* (June 2011). https://doi.org/10.1093/ije/dyq148

Harris did acknowledge that home life seems to be responsible for up to 5% of the personality variance of kids living under the same roof. See "Judith Rich Harris: 1938 - 2018" (January 9, 2019). https://www.edge.org/conversation/judith_rich_harris-judith-rich-harris-1938-2018

Harris' theory of peer group loyalty is well-detailed in her paper, "Where Is the Child's Environment? A Group Socialization Theory of Development" which appeared in *Psychological Review* (July 1995).

Robert Plomin's comment on parents mattering but not making a difference is elaborated in his 2018 book, *Blueprint*, and also in his article "Parents Matter but They Don't Make a Difference" (September 27, 2018): https://www. psychologytoday.com/us/blog/blueprint/201809/parents-matter-they-don-t-make-difference. Note that Plomin has a somewhat different take than Harris by emphasizing the relative importance of random events over peer socialization.

Picking Peers

See Chapter 7 of my book, *The Art of Self-Directed Learning*, for more about Deer Crossing Camp and the *T'naci* monster.

Anne-Marie Ambert's study is "A Qualitative Study of Peer Abuse and Its Effects: Theoretical and Empirical Implications" in *Journal of Marriage and Family* (2014). https://www.jstor.org/stable/352708

Ambert's quote was cited in Malcolm Gladwell's 1996 New Yorker piece, "Do Parents Matter?"

Jess Row's quote is from "How to Grant Your Child an Inner Life" (February 18, 2019). https://www.newyorker.com/culture/culture-desk/how-to-grant-your-child-an-inner-life

Browsing and Hanging Out, Reconsidered

Brendan Leonard's paean to YouTube is from "Thank You for YouTubing" (September 13, 2018). https://semi-rad.com/2018/09/thank-you-for-youtubing/

On the topic of sheltering, simply replace the word "television" with "YouTube" in this quote from *The Nurture Assumption*: "Preventing an individual child from watching television would not protect that child against its influence, because television's impact is not on the individual child—it is on the group. Like all other aspects of the culture, what is portrayed on the television screen will have long-term effects on an individual's behavior only if it is incorporated into the culture of the peer group. It often is."

For parents especially concerned about online culture taking their kids to dark places, I recommend reading "What Happened After My 13-Year-Old Son Joined the Alt-Right" (May 5, 2019). The parents in this article show that, while most enculturation is outside your control, it is possible to remain autonomy-supportive and accompany your kid's intellectual journey instead of clamping down on them. https://www.washingtonian.com/2019/05/05/what-happened-after-my-13-year-old-son-joined-the-alt-right/

Eyes on the Prize

Kim Brooks' quote is from "The Struggle To Reclaim Parenting" by Kim Brooks (April 21, 2015). https://www.buzzfeednews.com/article/kimbrooks/reclaiming-parenting

On the topic of modern society harshly judging parents who leave their children alone, consider a 2016 study in which researchers created a series of situations where a parent left a child unattended for some period of time. Participants in the study were then asked to judge the risk of harm to the child during that period. In one scenario, a 10-month-old was left alone for 15 minutes, asleep in the car in a cool, underground parking garage. In another scenario, an 8-year-old was left for an hour at a Starbucks, one block away from her parent's location. The researchers then altered the reasoning behind why the child was left unattended. In some cases, the child was left alone unintentionally (for example, in one case, a mother is hit by a car and knocked unconscious after buckling her child into her car seat, thereby leaving the child unattended in the car seat). In other cases, the child was left unattended so the parent could go to work, do some volunteering, relax or meet a lover. Unsurprisingly, parents were judged more harshly for leaving a child alone for intentional reasons (e.g., to meet a lover). The more shocking result was that participants considered these same children to be in significantly greater danger when left alone intentionally, even when the details (the age of the child, the time and place of sitting unattended) were held constant. Regardless of actual threats, if a parent intentionally let their child out of sight, that child was considered imperiled. See "Why Do We Judge Parents For Putting Kids At Perceived — But Unreal — Risk?" by Tania Lombrozo (August 22, 2016). https://www.npr.org/sections/13.7/2016/08/22/490847797/why-do-we-judge-parents-for-putting-kids-at-perceived-but-unreal-risk

I borrowed the distinction between loving one's children and loving the act of parenting from "All Joy and No Fun" by Jennifer Senior (July 2, 2010). http://nymag.com/news/features/67024/

Ben Hewitt's quote is from "The Case for Letting Kids Be Kids" by Ben Hewitt (September 1, 2018): https://www.outsideonline.com/2339656/case-letting-kids-be-kids

Alison Gopnick's quotes are from "A Manifesto Against 'Parenting'" by Alison Gopnick (July 8, 2016). https://www.wsj.com/articles/a-manifesto-against-parenting-1467991745

5: YOU CAN AFFORD TO RELAX ABOUT COLLEGE

Our Secular Religion

Imagine a small town where everyone believes that in order to live a prosperous life, they must attend church every Sunday. Because this belief is pervasive, many townspeople who want to be prosperous attend church. Those who don't care about being prosperous seldom attend.

Now imagine you're a parent who wants to give your child every advantage in life. You look around and see that the most successful townspeople, almost without exception, are devout churchgoers.

You have a skeptical friend who points out that church might not be *causing* these people's prosperity; it's simply a place where prosperity-seekers tend to congregate.

You understand your friend's argument—but you also want to play it safe. So you drag your kids to church every Sunday, because something must be happening there that makes people more prosperous, right?

This is our world.

It's no stretch to say that college is our modern secular religion. As iconoclast Peter Thiel once quipped, "Education may be the only thing people still believe in in the United States. To question education is really dangerous. It is the absolute taboo. It's like telling the world there's no Santa Claus."

There are three big reasons for our pervasive faith in college. The first reason is money. It's often thought that the more degrees you have and the better the universities you attend, the more money you will earn. Financially secure people tend to have college degrees, so we assume that degrees lead to financial security.

The second reason is enlightenment—developing a "life of the mind." Where else but college can you grapple with big ideas, encounter a diversity of opinions, and learn to think for yourself? If you want to become a cultured and intelligent member of society, then college is essential.

Finally, college is the easiest way to demonstrate your membership in the upwardly mobile middle-class. If you want to show the world that you've *made it*—i.e., you've reached the promised land, leaving deprivation behind—then college is your ticket. If you're the first member of your family to attend college, this applies doubly.

In this chapter, we will closely examine these claims. Does higher education actually lead to financial security? How, exactly, does college build a life of the mind? And how else might we think about "making it" today? Guided by two eminent thinkers—an economist and an English professor—we will build a common-sense framework for supporting your kid's college aspirations, or lack thereof. We will soothe the voice in your head that worries, despite the evidence we saw in Chapter 2, that you're forever damning your child by letting them step off the college-prep conveyer belt.

College is good for many things, but it is not the be-all and end-all. It does not have to be your religion.

What a Degree is Really Worth

Search online for the financial benefits of college, and you'll be instantly assaulted by a tidal wave of articles describing the pot of gold waiting at the end of the college rainbow. The specific numbers are always shifting, but more or less, a bachelor's degree is supposed to earn you an additional million dollars over your lifetime.

Yet it's equally easy to find college horror-stories today: the reports about ballooning tuition costs, crushing student loans, and recent graduates who can't find jobs.

As soon as you start digging, you begin to realize how elusive the answers about the financial benefits of college really are. "Wouldn't it be nice if someone analyzed all the relevant factors on this subject," you ask yourself. "Wouldn't it be great if someone gave me and my kid some straightforward, unadulterated advice on whether college is worth it, financially speaking?"

And then you discover Bryan Caplan.

Caplan is a professor of economics at George Mason University and someone who is fascinated by the question of college earnings. After years of blogging about the subject, Caplan decided to do a deep dive, where he measured everything that could be measured and came up with hyper-specific answers to the question "How much does a college degree earn you?" What emerged was his 2018 book, *The Case Against Education*, the most nuanced economic analysis of college earnings ever published.

Caplan's book is long, dense, and fascinating—and what he found isn't pretty.

*　*　*

Everyone knows that people with college degrees earn more money. Caplan doesn't disagree. On paper, the average college graduate earns 70% more over a lifetime than the average high school graduate, and the average high school graduate earns 30% more than the average high school dropout. But when Caplan investigated exactly when, how, and to whom these benefits accrued, he discovered that the big numbers we see in the news and share with our children concealed some shocking details.

We assume that young people steadily gain skills and knowledge through high school and college. This is what Caplan calls the "human capital" view—the idea that year by year, a student becomes gradually more competent and employable.

By this logic, a student who drops out after her third year of high school should be roughly three-quarters as competent as a high school graduate, and therefore she should capture three-quarters of the financial rewards of a high school graduate. Similarly, a college student who drops out after her second year should capture half the economic rewards of a four-year college degree. Yet, in reality, each of these people reap only a tiny fraction of the economic benefits.

Completing your final year of high school, for instance, offers a long-run financial boost that's bigger than all other years of high school combined. Completing your final year of college is even more impactful: that year alone is worth *twice* as much as the first three combined. (In both cases we assume that a student finishes in four years.)

The fact that graduates receive a huge financial premium upon graduating is a phenomenon that economists have known about for a long time; they call it the "sheep-skin effect," in reference to the fact that early diplomas were printed on sheepskin.

In light of the sheepskin effect, it doesn't make sense to hold a pure, human capital view of college. If college led to a steady increase of skills that employers rewarded with higher pay, then it stands to reason that an employer would think that an individual who completed 50% of a college degree would possess 50% of the alleged talent of a college graduate, and compensate accordingly. Yet this isn't what happens. Employers actually care about degrees a lot, which they demonstrate by paying a lot more for people who hold those little slips of paper.

Caplan offers a helpful thought experiment: From the point of view of maximizing your future work opportunities, would you rather have a Princeton education without the degree, or a Princeton degree without the education?

From the human capital view, you should obviously take the education—because what good is a degree if you don't have the skills to back it up? But most people will actually choose the degree, because most people understand that employers care more about degrees than they do actual skills—because beyond the basics, you can usually learn everything you need on the job.[27]

---

27 I shared Caplan's thought experiment on my Facebook page with some rather unconventional parents and young people. While many mused that a Princeton education might be fascinating, most said that they'd take the degree, simply because it opens so many doors. My favorite response was "take the degree and then go educate yourself elsewhere!"

This phenomenon holds true on the lower end of the economic spectrum, too. Why do bartenders, cashiers, cooks, janitors, and security guards earn significantly more when they possess a high school or college diploma—despite the fact that high school and college teach virtually no skills relevant to these jobs? Because of the sheepskin effect.

Caplan presents yet another problem for the human capital viewpoint: Why do students overwhelmingly dislike and avoid schoolwork? If there's a direct connection between learning and earning, then students should be happy to learn. Yet students of all ages are generally happy when a teacher cancels class. They like teachers who give easy As. They do as little work as possible in order to earn the highest grade.

From the human capital viewpoint, students should be upset when there's a snow day. They should prefer teachers who demand deeper learning. They should reject cheating as a senseless act. Yet this is mostly untrue. Why? Because most students intuit that the money is in the diploma, not the learning itself.

That's why an anxious high school student who doesn't get into his top-choice college might genuinely say, "I did all of this for nothing." High school is a means to an end, or as *The New York Times* columnist Frank Bruni puts it, "It's a performance. If the right audience doesn't clap, there was no point in even taking the stage."

The tragic part, Caplan's research revealed, is that students are right. Little substantive learning happens in school after a kid grasps the basics of reading, writing, and arithmetic. When a high school student asks, "When will I ever use this literature, algebra, or history in real life?" Caplan responds: You probably won't! Because it's not about the learning, it's about the diploma.

If so much of our education system doesn't actually build relevant job skills, why do employers love graduates so much? The answer lies in "job market signaling," another established concept in the world of economics. To "signal" is to show potential employers that you are a productive, diligent, and intelligent person who can play well with others, tolerate boredom, and conform to social norms.

In a mass society, signaling is useful because businesses don't have the time to deeply assess every job applicant. They need a quick way to find out if someone will show up on time, work hard, play well with others, dress appropriately, speak appropriately, and not try to start a revolution. High school diplomas and college degrees signal those qualities. The more "competitive" a high school or college, the more likely its graduates are to defer gratification, perform under pressure, and spend large parts of their days diving into complex and esoteric topics like international trade law. This is why a degree from an elite college opens so many career doors; it's essentially a giant neon sign flashing the message "Hire me, and I'll do anything you ask!" It shows employers that you went through hell to get that slip of paper, so you'll go through hell to get a paycheck, too.

Employers do need to hire people with actual skills, of course. A graphic design firm won't hire someone who's never used Photoshop before. But the question remains: if a graphic design firm is deciding between hiring two designers who demonstrate equal levels of skill in their equally impressive portfolios—one has a college degree, and the other doesn't—

why will an employer hire the graduate? Because of signaling.

All things considered, Caplan's calculations led him to estimate that a whopping 80% of the financial value of a college degree comes from signaling and 20% from human capital. This is a powerful claim, yet I find myself convinced, because signaling explains so much of the inanity of schoolwork. It even explains the 2019 U.S. college admissions scandal in which rich parents paid handsome bribes to test administrators and sports coaches to help their kids get into elite universities. It doesn't make sense to sneak your kid into a college that they can't handle academically—unless college is mostly about signaling.

The Case Against Education argues that, at the end of the day, formal education is more of a hiring tool for employers than a useful experience for students. The primary function of conventional high schools and colleges is to separate students into categories that employers can easily digest: fast or slow, diligent or lazy, conformist or contrarian. To "do well" in school amounts to expressing the personality traits and work habits deemed valuable by the workplace. School is really just one long test of your willingness and ability to sit down, take orders, and do your work—no matter what that work may be.

*   *   *

So, what's a college degree actually worth? The average answer may still be a million dollars over a lifetime, but now we're in a position to add some nuance.

The sheepskin effect is a gigantic factor. If your kid does three years of college, pays full-price for those years—whether through student loans, their own earnings, or your rapidly diminishing bank account—and then drops out before taking a degree, they are probably not on the path to reaping the million-dollar pot of gold at the end of the rainbow. Their situation might even be far worse, financially speaking, than if they had never attended college at all.

What Caplan calls "ability bias" is another uncomfortable but vital consideration. Caplan uses this term to represent the fact that some students show up at school *already possessing* the specific abilities (both personality traits and cognitive abilities) that schools reward and employers seek. Conventional school is biased, for example, toward kids with higher measured IQ and conscientiousness scores. A family's income matters too, as wealthier families can bolster their kids' signaling abilities by paying for services like test prep tutors. The kid who is advantaged by both genes and finances will be set up, from day one, to perform better in school than his less fortunate peers. When the game is rigged like this, Caplan urges us to consider, how fair is it to tell *everyone* that higher education (or even high school) is a worthwhile investment?

Caplan reveals even more statistical elephants in the room. Consider the difference in starting salaries between wildly different fields. How much will a petroleum engineer from MIT make compared to a child psychology graduate from an unknown public university? What about foregone earnings: the money and job experience that a young person might have accrued by working full-time instead of going to college? What about the economic benefit of meeting a future spouse in college? What about the better healthcare, better retirement benefits, and lower risk of unemployment that college degree-holders enjoy? What if you're someone who especially loves or loathes conventional school? Somehow Bryan Caplan finds a way to quantify every one of these factors, citing a dazzling array of academic papers, and crunching them all together in one grand spreadsheet.

To simplify his results and make concrete recommendations, Caplan employs four archetypes—the Good Student, Excellent Student, Fair Student, and Poor Student—which represent four broad groups of academic abilities, inclinations, and family backgrounds.

The prototypical Good Student is a single, childless, full-time student who attended public K-12 schools and possesses the same cognitive ability, character, and background as the average college graduate who does not pursue further degrees. The Excellent Student looks like the typical person with a master's degree. The Fair Student matches the typical high school graduate who doesn't try to go to college, and the Poor Student matches the typical profile of the average high school dropout.[28]

Caplan calculates that the typical Good Student who earns a bachelor's degree from an inexpensive public university will receive a lifetime earnings boost of roughly 20%, all things considered, compared to what they would have earned with only a high school diploma.

Twenty percent isn't as sexy as the "million dollars over your lifetime" figure, as the final number will quite certainly

---

28 Caplan admits that these profiles are synthetic and cartoonish, but they're handy tools for statistical analysis. And for the record, Caplan's prototypical Poor Student is not necessarily someone who lives in financial poverty.

be less than a million dollars. But this is clearly still a huge gain. In this way, Caplan confirms our general cultural narrative that a bright student will earn more with a four-year degree than she would without one.[29]

But that's just one case. What about everyone else? Caplan proceeds to crunch the numbers while considering every possible variable: type of student, quality of the college, category of major, financial aid, and completion rate. He summarizes his advice thusly:

> Go to college only if you're a strong student or special case. College is a square deal for Excellent and Good Students who follow three simple rules. First, pick a "real" major. STEM is obviously "real"; so are economics, business, and even political science. Second, go to a respected public school. It probably won't charge list price, and even if it does, you get your money's worth. Third, toil full time after graduation. Working irregularly after finishing college is like failing to harvest half the crops you plant.

Despite Caplan's hardheadedness, I do appreciate his directness:

> Those who stray far from these rules get burned. For weaker students, college is normally a bad deal. If you're a

---

29 I question two of Caplan's assumptions here. First, he assumes that the average family pays only $3,600 per year out-of-pocket for public college tuition (a figure he got from the College Board) and, second, he assumes that the average student pays nothing for room and board (because Caplan assumes that every student lives at home). When you crunch the numbers a second time (as Caplan does) taking into account higher total out-of-pocket costs (i.e., $30,000 per year), the college earning premium drops by more than half for Excellent and Good Students and becomes fully negative for Fair and Poor Students.

> Fair Student, go only if you're a special case. Will you major
> in something like engineering? Did an elite school mirac-
> ulously offer a cushy scholarship?. . .Then despite your
> spotty academic record, college may be for you. Otherwise,
> skip college and get a job. Poor Students, finally, should not
> go to college, period.

On one hand, Caplan's analysis is circular; he's saying that students who aren't fit for college shouldn't go to college. On the other hand, the message is a breath of fresh air for the simple reason that it questions our religious faith in the healing power of higher education. Not everyone is cut out for the college game. "Pushing college on the failure-prone majority is cruelly misleading," he laments. "You might as well urge them to buy lottery tickets because jackpot winners live in luxury."

Caplan is not alone in making these observations. A 2016 *Boston Globe* exposé on student debt, for example, reached a similar conclusion:

> In the universal campaign to propel more disadvan-
> taged students into college, few education officials seem
> willing to broach this sad, painful reality: If you come from a
> family of very limited resources and you're not going to be
> able to finish college, you'd be better off never going at all.

It's easy to call Caplan an elitist, but at the same time, he doesn't argue in favor of the elite universities. Instead, he urges students to find excellent public universities like the University of Virginia, the University of Michigan, or UC Berkeley. Even if your kid is ambitious and determined enough to get into an Ivy League, Caplan suggests, he might do even better at your local state university: "Picture all the faculty attention and support the University of Delaware would shower on a student good enough for Harvard."

So when does it make sense, financially speaking, to go to an elite university? If you're an Excellent Student from a low-income family, and an elite university offers you a generous fee reduction, then Caplan says: go for it! As *The New York Times* reported in 2018, while very affluent families pay around $70,000 a year to attend an elite college—including all tuition, room, and board—poor families only pay an average of $6,000. The economist Raj Chatty has furthermore discovered that low-income students who attend elite colleges have a much higher chance of reaching the top 1% of earners than similar students who attend excellent public universities.

At the end of the day, Caplan's message to young people in *The Case Against Education* is that four-year college is only a smart financial investment if you're already inclined toward academics, you attend a public institution where you pay modest fees, and you major in a field with high earning potential. For everyone else, his analysis shows that college offers a mediocre or bad deal. And for those with weak academic qualifications, those harboring an active distaste for school, or those who will be paying full price at a private institution, college is a flat-out horrible investment.

How to Give Up $35,000 a Year

Is higher education the safest path to financial security? The honest answer seems to be: it depends.

Caplan's research does confirm some of our cultural narratives (like the idea that college graduates generally earn more than non-graduates) while revealing others as deeply fundamentalist (like the idea that college is a smart investment for everyone). There are so many important factors to consider when addressing this question, and I deeply appreciate Bryan Caplan for bringing all these factors together in one place.

Yet.

I cringe at the thought of labeling teenagers as "Good Students" or "Poor Students" based on their IQ, grade point average, and measured personality traits. I would never advise a young person to avoid college simply because they have a less-than-perfect academic track record and they intend to major in the liberal arts. And I wholeheartedly reject the idea that, just because college is mostly about signaling, highly transformative experiences cannot take place there.

How can I simultaneously accept Caplan's analysis while rejecting his guidance? Perhaps because I did much of what Caplan suggested, and things didn't turn out anything like he predicted.

In the year 2000, I graduated with straight As from my California public high school. I got into UC Berkeley—one of the best-value public universities in the United States—when it charged the pre-recession tuition rate of $8,000 per year. I worked toward a STEM major in astrophysics. While I didn't end up with this degree, I worked hard, finished in four and a half years, graduated without debt (thanks, Dad!), and went straight into full-time employment.

By Caplan's estimates, my 18-year-old self faced excellent prospects for future earnings. Plug me into that spreadsheet, and off I go!

Yet my story turned out to be far more interesting than anything a spreadsheet might have predicted. Halfway through my astrophysics degree I became disillusioned with physics and stumbled upon the field of alternative education, which I delved into (in a very self-directed way) and became incredibly passionate about. I soon knew that I wanted to study this idea full time, so I designed my own degree, spent the next two years taking classes of my choice, and ended up graduating with a self-labeled degree in "Alternative Schooling and Science Education."

This was perhaps the least marketable degree that UC Berkeley has ever issued. While it did help me land my first post-college job (at AstroCamp, an outdoor science school in Southern California), the field of outdoor education is not exactly a lucrative one. Despite working full-time and year-round, my annual income hovered around $10,000 to $15,000 per year for many years after college.

Things picked up, financially speaking, in my later twenties after I'd started my travel company, published my first book, and started public speaking. Yet a quick glance at my tax returns reveals that, in my prime earning years from age 30 to 35, I still only made an average of $43,000 per year. This is approximately the same amount white men aged 25–34 (employed full-time, averaging all education levels) earned in the United States in 2019, according the Bureau of Labor Statistics.

To be clear: I deserve no sympathy. I made an economic choice by shifting my focus from astrophysics to alternative education. The median salary for adults with a bachelor's degree in education in the U.S. is $46,000. For those with a bachelor's degree in physics, it's $81,000—a whopping

$35,000 premium that I chose to forsake.

Had I stuck out my astrophysics degree for another two years and gone into a science career, maybe I'd have equity in a house today instead of just a used Subaru, a MacBook, and a nice sleeping bag. If I'd gone on complete a graduate degree in Physics, maybe I'd even be making the median income of such people—$101,000—and enjoying a more comfortable existence today.

But here's the thing: I love my life. If I had gone into science just for money's sake, I wouldn't be the same person I am today—and I really like the person I am today. I've been able spend more than 10 years earning money by traveling the world with enjoyable teenagers in tow. I've worked at summer camps I love, started my own businesses, and developed myself as a writer and public speaker. I wake up most mornings excited to hop out of bed and get to work. I've lived in beautiful places, built a wide network of friends, and gone on memorable adventures. And I've genuinely enjoyed the challenges of living an intentionally frugal life.

When I was at UC Berkeley, I witnessed the lives of astrophysics graduate students. They worked their butts off in front of a computer screen for 12 hours a day. Most didn't mind this schedule, because they genuinely loved their work. But while I found astrophysics fascinating, I soon realized that hardcore math and physics wasn't my calling. I wanted to be outdoors, I wanted to work with young people, and I wanted to work for myself—none of which would have been easy if I stayed on the track to become a scientist.

Choosing to study alternative education in college felt far more meaningful to me than studying esoteric cosmic phenomena and publishing academic papers that only a handful of other people would read. Working to abolish the needless suffering of young people stuck in an obsolete education system felt like a far more important mission.

Social scientists can measure many things, but they cannot measure everything. One of Bryan Caplan's spreadsheets could have never predicted what took place for me in college. And while I clearly failed to maximize my earning potential, I still feel like I made unequivocally important choices, ones that I won't regret on my deathbed.

It's clear that students who aren't a good fit for college shouldn't go, especially if they'll accrue debilitating student debt along the way. Yet at the same time, it's unequivocally foolish to ignore the non-economic potential of college: the enlightenment factor. Higher education still holds a special potential in our world, one that can dramatically shape someone's life for the better.

The Inestimable Value of College

Sometimes I imagine that Bryan Caplan has a long-lost twin: someone as quick-witted and insightful as he is, but someone who took a different life path that led to very different beliefs.

That metaphorical twin exists, and his name is William Deresiewicz. If Bryan Caplan is the patron saint of viewing higher education through the lens of economics, then William Deresiewicz is the patron saint of viewing higher education through the lens of enlightenment.

Deresiewicz studied English at Columbia University and taught English to undergraduates at Yale University. When his contract ended and he couldn't find a suitable job in academia, he moved to Portland, Oregon, and began writing powerful essays critiquing higher education in the United States. These essays struck a global nerve, leading Deresiewicz to publish his best-selling 2014 book, *Excellent Sheep*.

Inside the pages of *Excellent Sheep*, I discovered a devastating attack on elite universities in the United States, but I also found something I didn't expect—a love-letter to four-year college. Deresiewicz had written the most elegant and powerful defense of the broad, unspecialized, liberal arts college experience that I'd ever read: exactly the kind of education that Bryan Caplan considers wasteful for the vast majority of young people. Without a single spreadsheet or statistic, Deresiewicz argued for higher education's potential to enlighten, transform, and elevate a young person, and these arguments spoke directly to my personal experience.

Just as I adore Caplan's tear-down of higher education, I adore Deresiewicz's defense of it. Their two voices feel like a pair of angels and demons on my shoulders, each essential and irrefutable. Caplan had his turn. Now let's listen to Deresiewicz.

*   *   *

Deresiewicz's first claim is that college is essential for developing a life of the mind. Everyone can think, in a basic sense—but how do you learn how to think? Here Deresiewicz isn't talking about analytical skills like computer programming, but rather about developing a healthy sense of skepticism: "it means learning not to take things for granted, so you can reach your own conclusions."

The author of *Excellent Sheep* stands up for late-night

bull sessions, unstructured conversations, and other informal situations where students can shape the grains of sand that they received in the classroom into pearls of understanding. Where else but college can a young person grapple with ideas, full-time, in the presence of similarly motivated peers? In my own college experience, sometimes this looked like formal debates (like when I waded into the contentious waters of race, class, and gender in my education classes); sometimes it looked like a study group (like when my friends and I pulled our hair out over the same astronomy problems), and sometimes it resembled partially intoxicated rambling (like the 10 p.m. to 2 a.m. hours in the common area of my 125-person student cooperative house).

College professors also play a crucial role here. Young people arrive at college full of assumptions about how the world works, and a good professor drags these notions into the light, "precisely, patiently, responsibly, remorselessly." Professors insist that students defend their beliefs—or at least acknowledge that they're there—and thus give students a chance to think for themselves, "instead of merely being a receptacle for the thoughts of others."

I recall a course I took in international rural development policy, a subject in which I had no experience or special interest, in which I first learned about the World Bank, International Monetary Fund, and the other institutions that provide aid to developing nations. Whenever we read about a policy that sounded good on paper, the professor, Claudia Carr, told us to add the questions "for whom?" and "for what purpose?" to the end of the statement. Micro-loans are good...for whom? For what purpose? Developing natural resources is good…for whom? For what purpose? In other words, *cui bono*—who benefits? So much foreign aid, I began to see, actually benefited the donors more than the recipients. While I may have learned similar lessons by reading a book or watching Professor Carr's lectures online, there was something undeniably powerful about listening, in-person, to her heart-felt demands that I always ask these questions and that I not let myself be fooled. She burned the habit of skepticism into my brain. Other professors did this in their own ways, both at UC Berkeley and the community college I attended for a semester. None of my high school teachers even came close.

Learning to think skeptically is something that you don't just do to improve your own life, Deresiewicz argues—it makes the entire world a better place. A world of skeptics is a world you want to live in. Tara Westover, the homeschooled author of the best-selling book *Educated*, put it this way:

> Education should always be an expansion of your mind, a deepening of your empathy, a broadening of your perspective. It should never harden your prejudices. If people become educated, they should become less certain, not more. They should listen more, they should talk less. They should have a passion for difference and a love of ideas that aren't theirs.

Deresiewicz's next claim is that college helps you build a self, which he alternately calls a soul. He doesn't use that word in a religious sense, but rather to indicate that a powerful college experience will develop us morally, intellectually, sensually, and emotionally. Higher education should be an odyssey that incites, disrupts, and violates your notions of who you are. If you walk out of college the same person as you walked in, then you have failed, even if you're walking straight into a secure job:

> You need to get a job, but you also need to get a life. What's the return on investment of college? What's the return on investment of having children, spending time with friends, listening to music, reading a book? The things that are most worth doing are worth doing for their own sake. Anyone who tells you that the sole purpose of education is the acquisition of negotiable skills is attempting to reduce you to a productive employee at work, a gullible consumer in the market, and a docile subject of the state. What's at stake, when we ask what college is for, is nothing less than our ability to remain fully human.

It's very hard, Deresiewicz reiterates, to do this on your own. Why? Because college surrounds you with minds that are "looking for their own answers in their own ways," and this puts pressure on you to do the same.

Again, this all rings true for me. I walked into Berkeley as a nerdy, shy, introverted gamer who thought he wanted to be a scientist. I walked out a more extroverted, adventurous, and self-confident person with a burning passion for education. While some of these changes unquestionably arose from reading good books, working at Deer Crossing Camp, and some other activities that I may have done without college, I cannot deny that the peer pressure of 30,000 smart, searching minds hovering around me had a profound influence.

Finally, higher education makes you *interesting* as a person—but not in the way you might assume. Deresiewicz explains:

> Being a quadruple major does not make you interesting. Editing the college newspaper while singing in an a cappella group, starting a nonprofit, and learning how to cook exotic grains—this does not make you interesting. Interesting is not accomplished. Interesting is not "impressive." What makes you interesting is reading, thinking, slowing down, having long conversations, and creating a rich inner life for yourself.

Building a self or a soul isn't about building a résumé; it's about figuring out how to see *everything* as potentially interesting. This is why Deresiewicz believes that a broad, interdisciplinary liberal arts experience will almost always trump a narrow, technical course of training. "The idea that we should take the first four years of young adulthood and devote them to career preparation alone, neglecting every other part of life," he concludes, "is nothing short of an obscenity."

Deresiewicz argues that college has the power to give your life direction if you go about it the right way. We assume that top-rated colleges open unlimited doors for their graduates, career-wise. But where do most Harvard students actually end up? A survey conducted by the Harvard Crimson in 2018 discovered that 18% of graduates were going into consulting, another 18% into finance, and 14% into technology. Translation: 50% of those attending the most prestigious university in the U.S. were going into just three fields, all of which pay extremely well. Harvard may open many doors, but it may also condition its graduates to choose the most lucrative doors.

Do the graduates of elite colleges love their work? Deresiewicz suspects that they're simply following the options placed in front of them:

> When you walk into a Starbucks, you are given a choice between a latte and a Frappuccino and a few other things, but you also have another option. You can turn around and leave; maybe what you really want is not there at all. When you walk into an elite college, you are offered a choice between medicine, finance, consulting, and maybe a few other things, but you do not have to order from that menu, either. You can even turn around and leave and think it over for a while.

What does it take to walk out of the proverbial Starbucks, to walk away from most lucrative job offers that your diploma can buy? Deresiewicz argues that the right college experience builds *moral courage*, something that gives a young person the real power to determine their life path:

> The morally courageous person tends to make the individuals around him very uncomfortable. He doesn't fit with their ideas about the way the world is supposed to work, and he makes them insecure about the choices they themselves have made—or failed to make.

College helps you learn how to think. Learning how to think helps you build a self. Building a self gives you moral courage. And moral courage is what empowers you, the recent college graduate searching for his first job, to not just take the highest offer on the table. It helps you answer the derisive question, "So what are you going to do with *that*?" when you choose to study philosophy, history, education, or another non-lucrative field about which you may be passionately curious.

Following your curiosity is perfectly acceptable, Deresiewicz argues. "Vocation is Latin for calling," he reminds us. "It means the thing you're called to do. It isn't something that you choose, in other words; it chooses you. It is the thing you can't not do." Nor is studying a "worthless subject" self-indulgent. What isn't self-indulgent, Deresiewicz wonders, about going into finance, consulting, tech, or law? What makes studying history fundamentally more selfish than earning gobs of money at a corporate consulting firm? "It's selfish to pursue your passion, unless it's also going to make you a lot of money, in which case it isn't selfish at all." (Or, as the social critic Dwight Macdonald put it, "We think it odd that a man should devote his life to writing poems, but natural that he should devote it to inducing children to breakfast on Crunchies instead of Krispies.")

Deresiewicz tears apart the "Yale or jail" mentality that has come to dominate the American upper-middle class—the idea that you either attend a highly selective university or you end up at the bottom. In Deresiewicz's first viral essay, "The Disadvantages of an Elite Education", he reminds us how black-and-white that assumption is:

> You can live comfortably in the United States as a schoolteacher, or a community organizer, or a civil rights lawyer [...] that is, by any reasonable definition of comfort.

You have to live in an ordinary house instead of an apartment in Manhattan or a mansion in L.A.; you have to drive a Honda instead of a BMW or a Hummer; you have to vacation in Florida instead of Barbados or Paris, but what are such losses when set against the opportunity to do work you believe in, work you're suited for, work you love, every day of your life?

You *can* do purposeful work and enjoy basic economic security at the same time, Deresiewicz argues. Following your calling might be actually the best path to such security: "There's no use going into engineering if you aren't very good at it. You'll learn more, do better, try harder, and be more successful if you study something that you're interested in." (Can you see why I believe he's an unschooler at heart?)

Deresiewicz himself came from a family of Jewish immigrants, all of whom were professionals who valued science. In high school, he loved biology and was curious about psychology, so he majored in both at Columbia University. He didn't stop to think; he rushed right in. "By the time I realized that I should have been an English major, it was too late to make the switch." He did eventually attend graduate school for journalism, and then another graduate program for English. Even though he was an older student, the job prospects were slim, and he was initially rejected by 9 of the 11 programs he applied to, he had finally found his calling:

...for the first time in a very long while, I performed at the top of my ability, and for the first time ever, I loved being in school. I'd study for seventy, eighty hours a week, reading until 4 A.M. in my crummy little room in graduate student housing, and I had never been happier. I had finally learned to listen to my gut, or in more sophisticated terms, had come to recognize the moral significance of desire. I had found out that I could do what I wanted, and that I could do it just because I wanted to.

Following your calling is risky, he admits. For every George Eliot or Steve Jobs, many more fall short. "The reason to try, the reason to invent your life—whether you aim at remarkable things or only at your own thing—is so that it will be your life, your choice, your mistakes."

This makes me think of my own father, who at age 30 was earning a living fueling airplanes on the graveyard shift at Oakland Airport after working a string of short-term gigs as a glider flight instructor, towplane pilot, and campground manager in Big Sur, as well as serving for three years as an army officer in Germany and Vietnam. He'd earned a bachelor's degree in English from UC Berkeley after flunking out of Middlebury College. He decided then that if he wanted to enjoy his life, he had to work for himself. He resolved to start his own business or go down in flames trying. He stumbled upon an opportunity in the form of two ice cream machines imported from Italy, which he used to start a small ice cream manufacturing and retail business in San Francisco while still working the graveyard shift at Oakland airport. His first store, Gelato Classico, succeeded. He opened an equally popular second store and, three years later, sold the company for a sizable profit. His entrepreneurial gambit paid off in the end, but the whole thing could have failed at any moment, as he told me repeatedly when I was growing up. But if he had failed, he also told me, at least it would have been his failure—his life, his choice, and his mistakes.

If someone advises you to forget your passions and focus exclusively on financial security, Deresiewicz encourages, then ask yourself if that's what that person did with their life. "Chances are it's not, and if it is, ask yourself if they seem like a happy person." He insists that risks must be taken on the path to a meaningful life:

Parents tend to forget what it's like to be young, what youth can endure and achieve. How often have I heard of people telling their children not to take exactly the same kinds of risks—whether personal or professional, about work or sex or whatever—that they not only survived just fine themselves, but that made them who they are.

In other words, don't just do what your parents want. Don't just do what your peers are doing. Don't just do what's trendy at the moment. A broad-based liberal arts education, in Deresiewicz's mind, offers young people the best chance of saying no to these eternally powerful forces. It won't guarantee conventional success, but it will grant something far more important:

Instead of success, make the work itself the goal. That's what I always come back to. When I start to care too much about rewards, I remember to return to the work—to the never-ending effort to perfect it. Just put your head down and forget about everything else: happiness has come to me when I have done that, misery and false directions otherwise. . .Whether you get the recognition you think you deserve is out of your control, but the task itself is not. Aim high, to be sure, but do it for the love of the work. The work and the love—that's all that's going to be there in the end in any case. The only real grade is this: how well you've lived your life.

Putting it All Together

Can the economist and the English professor both be right? Can you take a hard-headed approach toward higher education's return-on-investment while also honoring its soul-building potential?

First, let's highlight where their advice overlaps. Caplan and Deresiewicz both recommend high-quality public universities over ritzy private universities. They also agree that only motivated students should attend, by which they mean intrinsic motivation.

Of course, how can we reasonably expect a young person to survive conventional schooling with their intrinsic motivation intact? High schoolers have been tested, graded, and otherwise browbeaten with extrinsic motivators for 12 years, as Deresiewicz masterfully explains in *Excellent Sheep*:

> The whole of childhood and adolescence, across a large swath of society, is now constructed with a single goal in mind. All the values that once informed the way we raise our children—the cultivation of curiosity, the inculcation of character, the instillment of a sense of membership in one's community, the development of the capacity for democratic citizenship, let alone any emphasis on the pleasure and freedom of play, the part of childhood where you actually get to be a child—all these are gone.

Meanwhile, in *The Case Against Education*, Caplan does eventually admit that going to college can be "good for the soul"—yet he believes that such enlightenment only takes place when high-quality teaching, high-quality content, and eager students co-exist. He is not confident that eager students exist in the first place:

> I embrace the idea of transformative education. I believe wholeheartedly in the life of the mind. What I'm cynical about is people. I'm cynical about students. The vast majorities are philistines. The best teachers in the universe couldn't inspire them with sincere and lasting love of ideas and culture.

Caplan is justified in his cynicism. (This is why self-directed learners who show "intellectual vitality" will always stand out.) But how much of young people's apathy is innate, as Caplan assumes, and how much is caused by the meat-grinder of school?

The education professor Kevin Currie-Knight observes that the college "philistines" that Caplan indicts are often the same individuals who invest large amounts of energy into non-school activities. They consume lots of arts and culture, just not the same arts and culture that Caplan values.

Currie-Knight sees the credentialing system itself as a more likely cause for student apathy:

> It may well be that students want to learn interesting things, but if school's primary value to them is to move through and gain a credential, that will affect what they do. If the goal is to maintain a high GPA, taking the intriguing but challenging course might lose out to taking the easier but potentially boring course. Students may want to spend time deeply pondering what they've just read, but if

their academic schedule is jam packed and they'd like to graduate, they will budget their time accordingly. If Caplan doesn't encounter many students who are intellectually curious, it may be that they really aren't, but it may also be that an education system where the primary goal is gain credentials just won't reward intellectual curiosity, so there's little use in exercising it there.

"Don't hate the players," Currie-Knight advises, "hate the game." Yes, school is mostly a signaling game. Yes, students do as little work as possible to get by. But does that necessarily mean most students don't crave a life of the mind? I'm not convinced. Even Caplan admits that, due to the expansion of school and the decline of free play over the twentieth century, college is now the first place where young people can truly relax and play:

> College gives students ample time for carefree exploration—time they rarely had in childhood. Plenty of undergrads fritter away their opportunity in a drunken stupor. Yet others sample a medley of fascinating options, acquiring passions that last a lifetime. My undergraduate years were my favorites precisely because classes were so undemanding. Every day was packed with hours for play, and play I did. I read philosophy, listened to opera, war-gamed with my friends, and argued politics with strangers past midnight. I owe my soul to lax academic standards.

Both Caplan and Deresiewicz argue that the right kind of person to attend college is one who wants to play with ideas, follow their curiosities, engage with their college community, and learn from their peers. The right kind of person has a highly developed system of intrinsic motivation. The right kind of person has thought hard about their decision to enter college instead of just following the crowd.

The right kind of person sounds awfully like an unschooler.

*   *   *

Many of the self-directed learners I know go to college, but they seldom dive straight into full-time academics when they're young. Instead, they gingerly test the waters by watching YouTube videos and going down Wikipedia rabbit holes. They develop budding academic interests—and then they go back to their games, sports, crocheting, or fan fiction for a while. Left to grow at its own pace, this tender green shoot of curiosity blossoms into a full-fledged interest. And then one day your kid walks up and tells you, "I want to sign up for a history class at community college." Another day they say, "I think I'm ready for university. What do I need to do to get there?"

It's so much harder to know if a kid coming from conventional school is serious about higher education, because she just finished running an academic marathon. Her motivational machinery needs rest and repair, having been fueled for too long by carrots and sticks. How can we expect her to know what's best for herself? How can we expect her to be emotionally honest about the prospect of another four years of full-time academics? How can we let her, in good conscience, take out student loans at this point in life, saddling herself with debt that would be unthinkable if it appeared on a credit card bill instead?

When your kid comes from conventional school, she has been swept toward college by a powerful tide of culture and peers. Is she genuinely ready and eager for college? Will she commit to finishing and not drop out early? Both she and you are gambling. Everyone likes to think of their children as above average, but if Bryan Caplan's statistics are to be believed, then there are more losers to be found in the college game than winners. Pushing an academically burnt-out and under-motivated 18-year-old into college is a poor bet on all accounts.

By giving your kid more autonomy in the K–12 years, you're lessening the likelihood that this situation will arise. You're letting your kid learn what intrinsic motivation feels like. You're letting him do at least *a few* things for himself— to stumble, to experience boredom, to consider different life paths—so that when society throws its religious proclamation of college-for-all in his direction, he won't respond with the knee-jerk "Yale or jail" panic.

You will never fully eliminate the risk of investing in college. Even some life-long unschoolers end up choosing college for the wrong reasons. But cultivating your kid's intrinsic motivation is the best hedge you can make against a wasteful or poorly timed college choice.

As a parent, you can offer your kid a variety of small-scale academic opportunities. Offer to sign them up for a biology class for homeschoolers, an online course taught by a popular history professor, a community college psychology course, or a summer camp that teaches coding through gaming. Play podcasts on long car rides. Strew interesting magazines around the house. Then you'll have a little information, at least, with which to gauge your kid's appetite and readiness for higher education. Forget the mythical age 18 deadline and give your kid a few extra years to make up their mind. Normalize the concept of gap years. College may be the largest outlay of time, money, and energy that your kid ever makes. Don't rush it.

What if your kid shows zero interest in every academic offering you make? What if their self-directed learning never leads them to say, "Hey mom, sign me up for community college?" Consider yourself blessed, because your kid is telling you that they're really not a good fit for four-year college. Not now, at least. This is a huge and largely undiscussed benefit of unconventional education. There are so many people in the world who clearly aren't a good fit for college, yet they carry the shame of not possessing a bachelor's degree far into adulthood. They believe they have missed the rite of passage, that they are unbaptized.

Much of this stigma is culturally created, so we cannot simply wish it away. But as a parent you can reassure your kid, through words and deeds, that you will love them regardless of the degrees they end up (or do not end up) receiving. You can help your kid find and explore the many wonderful occupations that don't require degrees. You can show them, over and over, that you're on their team—not the team of Conventional Success at All Costs. As William Stixrud and Ned Johnson, authors of *The Self-Driven Child,* eloquently put it:

> [If] you want your kids to succeed in life, don't perpetuate a fear-based understanding of success. Start with the assumption that your children want their lives to work. Then tell them the truth: That we become successful by

working hard at something that engages us, and by pulling ourselves up when we stumble.

If you want your kids to taste the fruits of higher education, then don't push them through the college prep meat-grinder. Instead, speak honestly to them about what you loved (or hated) about your own college experience (or lack thereof). Invite them to taste college life as much as possible before they ever begin a college application. Invite a hungry graduate student over for dinner and get her talking life in the ivory tower; the following week, invite someone who never went to college and turned out just fine. If you have a highly academic background yourself, ask yourself how you might inspire an appreciation for the "life of the mind" in your child without also saying that college is the only path.

Self-Directed Signaling

Finally, let's address the "boss level" challenge of supporting your kid as a self-directed learner. What if your 18-year-old doesn't go to college, doesn't get a high school diploma, and doesn't possess any marketable skills?

As Bryan Caplan made clear (and William Deresiewicz doesn't refute), job market signaling still matters. Sometimes it matters a lot. That's why the thought of raising a fully uncredentialed young person subdues many would-be supporters of alternative education. But this boss can be defeated.

Remember the fact that homeschoolers, unschoolers, and radical alternative schoolers overwhelmingly report that when their kids want to go to college, they *do* go to college. They don't necessarily end up at their first-choice institutions.

They don't necessarily go at age 18. But if they have an honest desire to attend a four-year college, they do get in. I've personally witnessed 19-year-old unschoolers with zero academic background—really, zero—pull one-eighties when they decided they needed to go to college. A year or two later, they're starting their freshman years. (Also recall that many self-directed learners begin doing college work *earlier* than normal.)

If you're concerned about your kid not possessing a high school diploma, take a moment to google the GED, HiSet, TASC, or a state-level high school equivalency exam. Based on the reports of previous unschoolers, these tests are straightforward. If your kid needs such a diploma to get hired, they can prepare for one these tests in a jiffy. The Clonlara School, based in Ann Arbor, Michigan, offers a time-tested way for non-traditional learners to obtain an accredited diploma—including those in countries where high-school equivalency exams don't exist.

Put the fear of raising a fully uncredentialed 18-year-old in context. Because the conventional school system is so pervasive, parents new to alternative education often set impossible standards for themselves. Remind yourself that many kids go to regular school, have a tough time there, and graduate learning virtually nothing. Many others drop out. Neither fate is desirable, yet neither is end of the world. Resources and programs exist to help such young people find gainful employment. If it helps, conduct a thought experiment: imagine that your kid was destined to rebel against the school system, learn nothing, and drop out. (Or simply graduate with a low GPA and unimpressive high school record.)

Now imagine all the pain and misery you helped them avoid by not forcing them to continue their schooling.

Inform yourself about the many highly paid career paths that don't require college degrees. A young person who is passionate about some aspect of computers or programming will always be employable. Yes, he might make less than his peers with four-year degrees. Yes, he might struggle more to get hired or contracted. But he will be employable.

Mike Rowe, host of the show *Dirty Jobs*, is a prominent public advocate for the skilled trades that have chronic job vacancies today, like plumbing, electrical work, welding, HVAC, carpentry, auto repair, construction, hairstyling, skin care, appliance repair, cooking, and baking. Highly credentialed parents may be quick to label these occupations as dead-ends; if that describes you, then I suggest you google Mike Rowe's writing, videos, and his "Works" Foundation. The jobs I listed above may even offer more security than your own career, in the sense that they cannot yet be outsourced or automated.

Finally, revisit the concept of gap years as a way of explaining to polite society that your kid is taking a bit more time to explore and become independent.

Caplan says that a college degree demonstrates a package of socially desirable traits—intelligence, conscientiousness, and conformity—and that it's difficult to signal just one or two of these traits. If, for example, you try to signal your intelligence by blogging about science fiction, then employers will wonder what "issues" stopped you from getting an English degree. If you try to prove your work ethic by copying the dictionary by hand, then employers will assume that you should have been able to handle four years of academic drudgery. Telling an employer that you're self-taught, Caplan warns, is a red flag for non-conformity. The further outside the box you go, the more your signal weakens. Employers want the package deal.

If your child is a nonconformist by nature, they will probably seek work in a nonconformist field, where employers care less about the package deal. But supposing Caplan is right, then I think that entrepreneurship is the best way for a self-directed learner to create their own signal. Running your own business shows that you're basically intelligent, conscientious, and conformist (in the sense that you will conform to other people's needs enough to get them to voluntarily pay for your product or service). In America we have a cultural soft spot for entrepreneurs that a savvy self-directed learner can take advantage of.

In my 2012 book, *Better Than College*, I shared the stories of unschooled young adults who created their own signals in lieu of college. Most took an entrepreneurial approach supplemented by volunteer gigs and unpaid internships. Although it is true that those without college degrees may struggle to find employment in government, banking, science, health, formal education, and other licensed and highly bureaucratic fields, they can always go back to college if they want.

Yes, signaling matters. No, uncredentialed young people cannot get any and every job with a snap of their fingers. Yet self-directed signaling is clearly possible. Taking an alternative path requires a bit more time and creativity, but fortunately those who take such paths often have more opportunity for that.

Diplomas are undeniably powerful, but the heavens do not fall for those who choose not to pursue our society's hallowed credentials.

Notes

For practical resources related to this chapter—and every other chapter in the book—please visit the book's dedicated webpage: https://blakeboles.com/y/

Our Secular Religion

The opening story was adapted, with permission, from my friend Isaac Morehouse's blog post: "Forget the Data, College is a Religion." (March 30, 2018). https://isaacmorehouse.com/2018/03/30/forget-the-data-college-is-a-religion/

Peter Thiel's quote is from "Peter Thiel: We're in a Bubble and It's Not the Internet. It's Higher Education." (April 11, 2011). https://techcrunch.com/2011/04/10/peter-thiel-were-in-a-bubble-and-its-not-the-internet-its-higher-education/

What a Degree is Really Worth

A typical article about college earnings looks like this: "A college degree is worth $1 million" by Quentin Fottrell (May 8, 2015). https://www.marketwatch.com/story/a-college-degree-is-worth-1-million-2015-05-07

All quotes and sources related to *The Case Against Education* are from the book's first edition (2018), unless otherwise noted.

My online thought experiment with the Princeton degree versus Princeton education: https://www.facebook.com/blake.boles/posts/10107808012347473

For more evidence against the human capital viewpoint, see David Labaree's book *How to Succeed in School Without Really Learning* (1997), where he argues that students use college primarily for social mobility, as well as Rebekah Nathan's book *My Freshman Year* (2005). Nathan (a pseudonymous anthropologist) goes undercover as an older freshman, noting how students talk about college largely in terms of procedural tasks and hoops to jump through, not as a place of learning.

For some evidence of how widespread cheating may be in high school today, see "I Was Part of a High School Cheating Mafia" by Andrew Fiouzi (2018). https://

melmagazine.com/en-us/story/i-was-part-of-a-high-school-cheating-mafia

On the 80/20 split between signaling and skills, Caplan admits that numbers are fuzzy, and the split may be less extreme in some cases. But signaling firmly takes the lion's share.

On the 2019 college admissions scandal (and Frank Bruni's quote), see "The Moral Wages of the College Admissions Mania" by Frank Bruni (March 16, 2019): https://www.nytimes.com/2019/03/16/opinion/college-admissions-scandal.html. And don't miss Caplan's take on it: "There's a Larger Lie Beyond the College Admissions Bribery Case" (March 14, 2019). http://time.com/5551315/college-bribery-larger-lie/

The Boston Globe piece is "The college debt crisis is even worse than you think" by Neil Swidey (May 18, 2016). https://www.bostonglobe.com/magazine/2016/05/18/hopes-dreams-debt/fR60cKakwUlGok0jTlONTN/story.html

On tuition differences for wealthy and poor families at elite schools, see "Top Colleges Are Cheaper Than You Think (Unless You're Rich)" by David Leonhardt (June 5, 2018). https://www.nytimes.com/interactive/2018/06/05/opinion/columnists/what-college-really-costs.html. The number cited in that article, $6,000, may even be high, as many selective colleges now offer full-ride scholarships (including tuition, room, and board) for families earning under $65,000 a year.

Raj Chatty's research is summarized in the article "Does It Matter Where You Go to College?" by Derek Thompson (December 11, 2018). https://www.theatlantic.com/ideas/archive/2018/12/does-it-matter-where-you-go-college/577816/

More on the special boost that low-income and minority students receive at elite colleges: "How Much Does Getting Into an Elite College Actually Matter?" by Kevin Carey (March 15, 2019). https://www.nytimes.com/2019/03/15/upshot/elite-colleges-actual-value.html

How to Give Up $35,000 a Year

Bureau of Labor Statistics, "Median usual weekly earnings of full-time wage and salary workers by age, race, Hispanic or Latino ethnicity, and sex, third quarter 2019 averages, not seasonally adjusted" (last modified October 16, 2019 / accessed December 1, 2019). https://www.bls.gov/news.release/wkyeng.t03.htm. I multiplied the figure for white men ages 25–54 ($1,070/week) by 50 weeks to get $41,200.

The median salaries for degrees in Education and Physics are from "The Economic Value of College Majors" by Anthony P. Carnevale, Ban Cheah, and Andrew R. Hanson (2015 / accessed December 1, 2019). https://cew.georgetown.edu/cew-reports/valueofcollegemajors/#explore-data

The Inestimable Value of College

Deresiewicz's most popular essays are "The Disadvantages of an Elite Education" and "Solitude and Leadership," both available online at *The American Scholar.*

All quotes and sources related to *Excellent Sheep* are from the book's first edition (2014).

Contrary to popular assumption, Deresiewicz didn't leave Yale because he was denied tenure; he simply couldn't find a suitable job in academia: "William Deresiewicz Talks with Executive Editor, Frank Shushok, Jr. about His Book, *Excellent Sheep: The Miseducation of the American Elite & the Way to a Meaningful Life*" (December 4, 2017). https://onlinelibrary.wiley.com/doi/full/10.1002/abc.21301

It's worth noting that Deresiewicz is highly skeptical of autodidacts. As he wrote in *Excellent Sheep*: "There may be brilliant autodidacts out there, people who need nothing but the world and a library. . .but they're almost as rare as the Gateses and Zuckerbergs. Even Thoreau, the archetypal nonconformist, went to college, and may not have been Thoreau if he had not. It's true that college is imperfect even in the best of situations. Soul-making will never be strictly compatible with syllabi and semesters; imagination and courage do not fit neatly within rules and requirements. But if getting an inadequate education is bad, then getting none at all is even worse. You need to get a base, before you can take off on your own." For a more nuanced discussion about this topic, find my 2019 podcast interview with Deresiewicz, "The Power and Peril of Self-Education." https://soundcloud.com/blakebo/bill-deresiewicz-on-the-power-and-peril-of-self-education

Tara Westover's quote is from "She Never Saw A Classroom Until College. Now She Has A Ph.D. And A Lot Of Thoughts About Education" by Catherine Brown (August 27, 2018). https://www.forbes.com/sites/catherinebrown/2018/08/27/she-never-saw-a-classroom-until-college-now-she-has-a-ph-d-and-a-lot-of-thoughts-about-education/

The Harvard Crimson webpage is "The Graduating Class of 2018 by the numbers" (undated, accessed December 1, 2019): https://features.thecrimson.com/2018/senior-survey/after-harvard-narrative/

Dwight Macdonald's quote is from *Excellent Sheep* (2014).

Deresiewicz's quote "You can live comfortably in the United States as a schoolteacher…" is from "The Disadvantages of an Elite Education" (June 1, 2008). https://theamericanscholar.org/the-disadvantages-of-an-elite-education/. I removed the word "artist" at his request.

Putting It All Together

While Caplan and Deresiewicz both advocate for high-quality public universities, Deresiewicz additionally advocates for a certain type of ritzy private college: small liberal-arts colleges like Reed, Kenyon, Wesleyan, Sewanee, and Mount Holyoke. These are schools you won't see near the top of the U.S. News and World Report college rankings, but you may easily find in alternative directories like *Colleges That Change Lives*, *Hidden Ivies*, or the *Washington Monthly College Guide and Rankings*. Deresiewicz believes that they're the perfect environments for soul-building because of their small classes, professors who are committed to teaching (instead of research), and the fact that students enjoy more of a voice in important campus matters.

"Review of Bryan Caplan's The Case Against Education" by Kevin Currie-Knight (August 17, 2018) in the *Journal of Value Inquiry*. https://doi.org/10.1007/s10790-018-9640-2

Self-Directed Signaling

Deresiewicz's take on America's entrepreneurial soft spot: "Generation Sell" by William Deresiewicz (November 12, 2011). https://www.nytimes.com/2011/11/13/opinion/sunday/the-entrepreneurial-generation.html

6: ALL THEY WANT IS CONNECTION

What I Learned at Not Back to School Camp

Late one summer evening, I found myself driving the tree-lined streets of Eugene, Oregon. With one hand clutching the steering wheel and the other clutching Google Maps—this was in 2006, when one still printed driving directions on paper—I scanned the dark streets for house numbers.

I had just driven 10 hours from the mountains of California. It was my first time in Oregon, and I was about to start a brand new summer camp job, just one day after completing a full summer working as the assistant director of Deer Crossing Camp. A frothy brew of excitement, nervousness, and exhaustion sloshed around in my stomach.

I found the house, and inside, my soon-to-be fellow camp counselors. One by one they stood up and gave me a hug.

But the star of show—the camp director, the famous author—wasn't there.

Grace Llewellyn was out dancing tango.

A half-hour later, she returned, beamed me a smile, and gave me a sweaty hug. In one hour, I had already received more hugs from the staff of Not Back to School Camp (NBTSC) than I had from anyone in the three preceding months.

The next morning, we began our first staff meeting with a check-in. Coming from the world of traditional summer camps and outdoor education programs, the only type of check-in with which I was familiar was the logistical variety: Are all the kids accounted for? What are my responsibilities for the day? Do we have all the supplies we need? What's the plan? At NBTSC, however, a check-in was a chance to reflect upon your entire being. How are you doing? How are you *really* doing? What's up for you? What's pulling you down? What's keeping you from being here and now?

As we went around the circle in Grace's house, each staff member shared from their heads and hearts. Some check-ins were quick and factual; others involved long periods of Quaker-like silence. Some people cried. More than once I found myself sitting through multi-minute monologues about the stresses, anxieties, relationship issues, health statuses, and philosophical musings of a co-worker whom I hardly knew.

In those first few days, my gut told me that these check-ins were unprofessional, an exercise in over-sharing, and a waste of precious time. Why weren't we discussing the workshops we were going to run, the principles of unschooling, or risk management policies? We checked-in twice a day, which often felt like two times too many. But I was new, I liked my co-workers, and I didn't want to ruffle feathers—so I played along, always keeping my own check-ins brief.

Soon my skepticism softened. In my previous workplaces there had always been a clear line between work life and personal life. At NBTSC, we discarded such compartmentalizing. Check-ins offered a window into the lives of my fellow staff that initially felt voyeuristic but soon revealed itself as an empathy-building tool. I felt the vulnerability and openness of our daily sharing starting to transform me.

Check-ins offered a powerful platform for debriefing stressful incidents, big and small. Halfway through the camp session, for example, there was a freak medical incident that I tackled as the camp's first aid authority. A 16-year-old camper had started acting weird and out of character. She began saying inappropriate things to campers and staff alike. I drove her to the local emergency room (accompanied by another staffer) where she was promptly admitted. Ten minutes later, I looked out the window and saw her wandering the hospital parking lot; she had apparently just gotten up and left the ER. The nurses guided her back inside where they promptly scanned her brain and discovered a small, spontaneous hemorrhage in her frontal lobe. This "brain bleed" was putting pressure on her decision-making and language-filter systems, causing her to act irrationally. They rushed her to another hospital where she received an operation and fully recovered within the next few days.

This wasn't my first medical incident, but it was by far the strangest. The following evening, at staff check-in, I shared a lot about the anxiety, stress, and confusion I felt during the incident. Previously I would have buried these emotions in the name of professionalism, but after many days of ritualized check-ins at NBTSC, I knew that my fellow staff would gracefully listen with full attention. No one would resent my "over-sharing," and no one would be checking their phones or whispering in side conversations. At every check-in—not just exceptional days like this—I knew that I would have the group's full, loving attention. This was a brand new experience for my 23-year-old self, and on this weird and stressful day, I witnessed its full power.

More cracks appeared in my emotional shell as I saw what this same check-in culture did for teenagers. At Not Back to School Camp, every advisor is responsible for an "advisee group" of approximately a dozen campers. Advisee groups are purposefully designed to combine young people of all ages (13–18), genders, and camp tenure (first-timers and old-timers). As an advisor, I was free to lead whatever games, discussions, or activities I pleased with my advisee group for the 30 to 60 minutes we met each morning—but starting with a check-in was mandatory. Grace was adamant about this. In a summer camp that gave teenagers many degrees of freedom, she explained, check-ins ensured that every individual camper was seen, heard, and acknowledged by an adult, every day. The advisor-advisee relationship was vital for ensuring that no one slipped through the cracks or felt overwhelmed in this high-freedom and high-responsibility camp environment.

With the foundation of a daily check-in, every camper at NBTSC—especially the newer, shyer, and more vulnerable ones—soon felt at home. Later, by the end of a 1- or 2-week session, the campers were positively gushing about how *connected* they felt to each other, to the staff, and to themselves.

But what did that word connection mean? I had previously worked in three other summer camps and two outdoor education centers, but connection wasn't yet a part of my lexicon.

I didn't have the words for it then, but what I observed in those grassy fields in Oregon was a massive, rapid infusion of something very important into the lives of young people who desperately craved it. Connection was the blood that coursed through the veins and arteries of Not Back to School Camp. It was the legal drug in which they trafficked.

I'll provide another example. A game that I picked up at NBTSC, and one I always play with my advisees, is called hot seat. When I first played it, hot seat just felt like a game of truth or dare, minus the dare. But it didn't take me long to witness the firepower of this fully armed and operational connection-generator.

Hot seat requires a group of a dozen-or-so teenagers who know a little bit about each other but aren't close friends. (NBTSC advisee groups and Unschool Adventures groups are perfect candidates.) I begin by asking for a volunteer to sit on the metaphorical hot seat, in which the teen agrees to answer every question asked of her for a defined period of time, usually 2 to 3 minutes. (If a camper really doesn't want to answer a question, they don't have to, of course.)

Next, I explain to the rest of the group that they are responsible for coming up with questions to ask the person on the hot seat. A great hot seat question should be something you're genuinely curious about. It should be something the person can answer in a brief amount of time. And crucially, it should be something that wouldn't be appropriate in normal, day-to-day conversation. This ensures that hot seat doesn't waste our time with boring, toothless questions like "What's your favorite color?" or "What did you eat for breakfast today?" If a hot seat question doesn't make you sweat a little, it's probably not a good question.

I then suggest a few broad categories that often lead to

good questions: dreams and fears, romance and sexuality, religion and spirituality, personal image, and family matters. For example, a few solid hot seat questions might include:

- What do you think will happen to you after you die?
- What do you wish was different about your relationship with your parents?
- What's one way you feel that your nontraditional education has failed you?
- If you could change one physical feature of your body, what would it be and why?
- If you could take one person at camp out on a semi-platonic picnic lunch date, who would it be?
- Do you have a camp crush? (And the perennial follow-up question: Who is it?)

I give the group a few moments to think up initial questions. I ask the volunteer if she's ready. I start the timer, and we're off! The volunteer receives a rapid-fire series of highly penetrating questions, asked popcorn-style, for a few minutes. She does her best to answer them, and then it's over. Ready for the next volunteer. Hot seat demands courage and vulnerability (when you're the volunteer), along with tact and creativity (when you're coming up with questions). It benefits from an experienced facilitator—typically a staff member or an older camper—who will maintain a serious tone and veto bad questions.

Advisee groups at NBTSC start as collections of strangers who are reluctant to talk to each other. But after a few days—and especially after a few rounds of hot seat—these once awkward, isolated, or nervous teenagers are now joking with each other, striking up deep conversations, and making plans outside of the group. They're connected.

One more powerful Not Back to School Camp activity that I'll highlight is a ceremony that I've witnessed nowhere else in the world. On the third evening of camp, most of the camp gathers in a large room and a facilitator divides them into two groups. One group spreads out to fill the majority of space in the hall, standing with their eyes closed and their hands by their sides. The other half is then free to walk around the room and give hugs to those with their eyes closed. (There are clear instructions and monitoring to ward off silly or inappropriate hugging.) After roughly 20 minutes, the huggers return to their side of the room, the huggees open their eyes, and then the roles reverse.

The first time I participated in this "bonding night" ceremony, I had no idea what to expect. I kept my guard up. Is this okay? Is it appropriate for these teenagers to be hugging me (and vice versa)? Once the little risk-management-officer who lives in my head determined that this was, in fact, a harmless activity, I let myself sink into it.

Have you ever received anonymous hugs from 50 people? Neither had I, and it created a feeling I'll never forget. Shivers were running up and down my spine. A wide smile hung on my face. I felt overwhelmed by love, acceptance, and gratitude. While I may jokingly refer to the evening rituals at NBTSC as "hippie bonding activities," I cannot deny their power. At every session of camp, without fail, ceremonies like this transform the young people at NBTSC from a loose group of individuals into a community positively pulsing with connection.

Why am I telling you all this? I'm not trying to convince you to send your kid to NBTSC. First of all, it's against the rules to be sent to NBTSC; all campers must attend camp voluntarily. Second of all, I don't know your kid. Maybe his personal nightmare is getting hugged by dozens of strangers and being asked to share his feelings every morning! Connection comes in different flavors, and Not Back to School Camp has mastered just one version of it—one that seems to work particularly well for unschooled and nonconformist teenagers.

My intention here, at the end of our journey, is broader.

Soon your child will be grown and forget about all this school and education business. He will have his own life, work, and relationships to worry about. Formal education constitutes just one episode of our (hopefully long) lives, and the details fade fast. I don't remember the vast majority of my grades, assignments, or test scores from school. Nor do you, I assume. We tend to forget what others say and do, but never how they make us feel.

What I've seen in my 15 years in the field is this: Whatever "connection" is, it's what young people crave, it's what they benefit from, and it's what they remember. With connection, everything is possible—learning, relationships, growth, you name it. Without connection, everything is difficult, and everyone goes home frustrated.

The Kids Aren't Alright

The world has improved in countless ways over the past century: fewer children die young, age-old diseases have been defeated, and safe water and sanitation are commonplace.

But there is one aspect of modern life that seems to be getting worse. Rates of anxiety and depression are rising, especially in wealthier countries, and especially among young people.

Consider the College Freshman Survey conducted by UCLA. In the late 1980s, when the survey began, about 20% of first-year U.S. college students reported feeling "overwhelmed by all I had to do" in the previous year (i.e., in their final year of high school). By the late 1990s, that number rose to 30%. By 2016, it hovered around 40%.

These surveys don't necessarily indicate rising stress or anxiety levels; they may instead indicate how comfortable people are talking about their stress and anxiety. With a steadily increasing awareness and acceptance of mental health, is it possible that such reports are just an artifact of a more sensitive and open society?

Jean Twenge, a psychologist from San Diego State University who focuses on generational differences, tackled this concern by studying the psychopathology of young Americans between 1938 and 2007 while controlling for "response bias," the tendency for earlier generations to downplay or lie about a taboo subject. She found that, despite changing cultural norms, roughly 5 to 8 times as many high school and college-aged young people met the criteria for clinically significant anxiety or depressive symptoms than those half a century ago.

In the twenty-first century, the story of mental health changes among young people is even less cheery. Between 2011 and 2015, a U.S. government survey reported a 50% jump in the number of teens demonstrating clinical depression symptoms. Another prominent survey of college undergraduates showed reports of "overwhelming anxiety" jumping from 51% in 2011 to 63% in 2018.

Perhaps most alarmingly, between 2008 and 2015, the number of teenagers admitted to U.S. children's hospitals for thoughts of suicide or self-harm doubled, with the majority of incidents taking place during the school year. During the same period, the suicide rate doubled for girls age 15 to 19. Between 2007 and 2015, among girls age 12 to 14, the suicide rate tripled.

In the very big picture, it's still a wonderful time to be a young person living in a prosperous country. You have clean drinking water, you're less likely to die from cholera, and you won't spend your days in a textile mill. And not all the news is bad—teenager's reported happiness levels in the U.S., for example, have remained consistently high in recent decades. Yet these facts offer little solace to the parent of a child whose anxiety and depression symptoms are creeping ever upward. Even if you aren't one of these parents, it's distressing to know that your kid's friends may be more anxious and depressed, considering how significantly peers shape each other.

What's causing all this anxiety and depression? What can be done? And where does connection enter the picture?

Meet Johann Hari

Johann Hari swallowed his first antidepressant when he was 18 years old. This was the late 90s, when commercial antidepressants had just begun flooding the global market. Hari, who had experienced chronic anxiety and unexplainable bouts of crying since he was a child, recalls that fateful meeting with his doctor in London:

In his little office, he explained patiently to me why I felt this way. There are some people who naturally have depleted levels of a chemical named serotonin in their brains, he said, and this is what causes depression—that weird, persistent, misfiring unhappiness that won't go away. Fortunately, just in time for my adulthood, there was a new generation of drugs—Selective Serotonin Reuptake Inhibitors (SSRIs)—that restore your serotonin to the level of a normal person's. Depression is a brain disease, he said, and this is the cure.

The doctor told him that his new drug, Seroxat (known as Paxil in the U.S.), would take two weeks to kick in. But that first evening, he felt a "warm surge" running through him, "a light thrumming that I was sure consisted of my brain synapses groaning and creaking into the correct configuration."

The Seroxat worked. In his first few months at university, Hari felt unusually resilient and energetic. Despite the side effects—he was putting on weight and sweating unexpectedly—he didn't feel sad anymore. But eventually the negative feelings returned, and Hari returned to his doctor, who prescribed a higher dosage. This cycle repeated:

So my 20 milligrams a day was upped to 30 milligrams a day; my white pills became blue pills. And so it continued, all through my late teens, and all through my twenties. I would preach the benefits of these drugs; after a while, the sadness would return; so I would be given a higher dose; 30 milligrams became 40; 40 became 50; until finally I was taking two big blue pills a day, at 60 milligrams. Every time, I got fatter; every time, I sweated more; every time, I knew it was a price worth paying.

By now, Hari was a successful journalist who wrote newspaper articles about depression. In these articles, he recited the simple formula he knew so well: depression is a disease of the brain, SSRIs are the cure—and thank god for them.

Only in his early thirties did Hari begin to question this formula. Why did his anxiety and depression perpetually return? If his symptoms were due to a chemical imbalance, why didn't his brain ever achieve balance? Why were antidepressant prescriptions skyrocketing? Everyone seemed to be anxious and depressed all of a sudden. Why was this happening *now*, in the beginning of the twenty-first century? Having recently finished a popular book about the war on drugs, Hari refocused on these questions—a quest that ended up consuming three years of his life. One of the discoveries that shocked him most was the power of the placebo effect, which accounts for much (but not all) of the effectiveness of antidepressants. Ultimately, he realized that his story was not unique at all, as some 65% to 80% of people on antidepressants continue to suffer from depression, year after year. Hari published his discoveries in his renowned 2018 book, *Lost Connections*.

Hari doesn't deny that genetics, brain chemistry, or childhood trauma play important roles in depression and anxiety. He doesn't tell anyone to abandon their medications or fire their therapist. But in *Lost Connections*, Hari does argue that the vast majority of depressive symptoms cannot—and should not—be attributed to uncontrollable biological and psychological forces. Instead, it is the social environment that holds the most power to address mental health challenges, an environment he explains through six "connections":

connection to meaningful work, connection to other people, connection to meaningful values, connection to status and respect, connection to the natural world, and connection to a hopeful or secure future.

When I discovered Hari's research, little alarms started going off in my head, because his "lost connections" so closely mapped onto young people's complaints about school—and the solutions he proposed closely resembled what Not Back to School Camp offered to teenagers.

You cannot change the school system yourself, but you can support your kid's choice to stop attending conventional school. In the same way, you cannot control the rising anxiety and depression of an entire generation of young people, but there is much you can still do for your kid to help them buck the trends.

Here, at the end of our journey together, I will borrow Hari's framework to offer six final pieces of advice to help your kid feel connected, stay engaged, and make it to adulthood with their mental health intact.

Six Connections

Connection to Meaningful Work

Hari observes that "meaningful work" requires feeling both a sense of purpose and a sense of control over your work. Self-directed learning advocates (myself included) frequently encourage young people to find their passions and pursue their interests, which certainly builds a sense of purpose. But considering the importance of also having a sense of control, there's an interesting counterargument to be made: when looking for work, perhaps a young person should care slightly less about passion and slightly more about finding a field where they can rapidly build skills and enjoy high control over their work.

There's some logic here. Perhaps it's better to be a highly competent accountant than a starving artist who gets treated like junk in her part-time service job. Perhaps not. Encourage your kid to seek their purpose *and* develop enough competency to enjoy real control over their work lives. Or, as I outlined in *The Art of Self-Directed Learning*, help them seek the intersection between passions (what feels purposeful), skills (where your competency lies), and the market (what people will actually pay for). That's where meaningful work is found.

Connection to Other People

Community doesn't just mean "being around other people," because you can be surrounded and still feel desperately alone. In *Lost Connections*, Hari reminds us that feeling connected to other people is about sharing things that matter with them on a regular basis.

This is why peer communities matters so much—and why there is a grain of truth in the ever-present "socialization" critique of homeschooling. I've witnessed diehard unschoolers willingly tromp off to conventional school just to have access to flesh-and-blood peers. Can you blame them? If it's a choice between making friends and being a self-directed learner, most kids will choose the former. At least school gives you something to complain about together.

All this is to say, respect your kid's need for social

connection, whichever direction it takes them. If they choose to attend conventional school against your wishes, so be it. If they make their best friends through online gaming, so be it. Your kid simply wants to share things that matter with other kids.

Connection to Meaningful Values

If extrinsic motivators make people anxious and depressed—which they do, as Hari extensively documents—then the implications are clear. Get your kid away from environments that revolve around "junk values": grades, money, popularity, and advertising.

This is tricky, of course, when you also want your kids to self-direct. Given free rein on YouTube, any kid will undoubtedly pick up materialistic notions that lead to negative consequences for their mental health. Censorship is unlikely to be effective; if they don't pick these values up directly from YouTube, they'll get them from their friends. A certain degree of fatalism is acceptable here. Yet there is one thing you can certainly do: increase your kid's access to play.

Peter Gray argues that the long-term decline in young people's mental health suspiciously parallels the long-term decline in children's free play. The more chances we give kids to play freely, both indoors and outdoors, the more intrinsic motivation, emotional regulation, and "internal locus of control" they'll develop, he argues, all of which combat anxiety and depression.

Of course, kids need a place to play, and they need other kids with whom to play. Gray believes that the solution lies in local neighborhoods. From the fifties to the eighties—before intensive parenting killed the party—kids were able to freely roam their own streets unsupervised. Today, an unsupervised group of kids may prompt a call to the police. Like a social network, a local neighborhood needs a critical mass of kids to support a culture of free play, and this begins with parental beliefs.

An organization that Gray co-founded, Let Grow, is working to combat the myths around children's safety and help individual communities band together to promote free and unsupervised play. If you nostalgically recall your own days as a carefree child playing in the neighborhood streets with your friends (as I do) and suspect that it connects to broader cultural values (as Peter Gray does), you can take action in your own community. Visit LetGrow.org.

Connection to Status and Respect

Social hierarchies are found in many parts of life—workplaces, friend groups, school groups, neighborhoods, and countries—and they all have one thing in common. It's miserable to be on the bottom.

I vividly remember my first day of public middle school in California. Everyone in the grassy common area was standing in a circle of friends, and I wasn't. My gut told me that I had to join one of these circles. So I attached myself to the "skater" clique—I'm talking about skateboarders, not those lowly rollerbladers—and did my best to fit in.

Despite my earnest efforts, I never got very good at skateboarding. I could ollie up a curb but not grind a rail or land a kickflip. This made me a poser: someone who dressed and talked like a skater but lacked any real skill. Guilty as charged. Despite this fact, the skaters let me hang around for a few years.

One day in ninth grade, after that same skater clique migrated to high school together, a strange and terrible thing took place. The leader of the group decided, for reasons never revealed, to kick me out the group. It was swift and brutal move. I arrived at school one morning and no one would talk to me. When I tried to approach a circle, they would close me out and turn their faces away.

My skater status was revoked, and I was thrust into the frigid hinterlands of high school society.

I did make new friends (those who shared my nerdy love of gaming) and survived the episode with my mental health intact. But I'll never forget the acute trauma of getting pushed out of the tribe and kicked down to the lowest rung.

If your kid is suffering social trauma as a direct result of their schooling, it's probably worth pulling them out. Spending too much time as someone else's punching bag constitutes an existential threat to one's mental health. On the other hand, the human world *is* one of social hierarchies, and each of us must learn how to dance among them.

This doesn't mean that every kid should attend their local conventional school as some sort of hierarchy-survival bootcamp, or that we should give grown adults mandatory jail time to teach them how the "real world" works. Recall the distinction between positive stress, tolerable stress, and toxic stress. Avoiding *all* stress isn't the answer. You want your kid to experience the *positive stress* of navigating social hierarchies. That can be fully achieved through alternative schools or mixed-age groups of homeschoolers or unschoolers.

Any group of young people can be vicious and exclusionary. Homeschoolers can still form cliques, though it's not as common as in conventional school. To the extent that we treat children like trapped animals, they will act like trapped animals—toward each other, and toward the adults in control.

Self-directed learners enjoy powers and privileges that conventional students could only dream of. Just imagine having the freedom to walk out of a class that you don't enjoy or voting on which staff to hire at your democratic free school. The status and respect afforded to young people in unconventional educational settings goes a long way towards promoting positive mental health.

Connection to the Natural World

The more access to green space that you enjoy, the less likely you are to suffer symptoms of depression and anxiety. This may be one simple reason that homeschoolers and alternative school students enjoy their lives: they don't have to ruefully stare out the windows on beautiful days like their brethren in conventional school. They simply walk outside.[30]

What if your kid shows no interest in nature? What if they just want to stare at computer screens all day? This is a common concern, and I align with Peter Gray's take on the matter, which he describes in *Free to Learn*:

---

30 Of course, for every alternative school surrounded by large grassy fields, there is another dwelling in a dark church basement. Homeschooling, too, can be its own kind of prison if your kid has no good access to nature. That's when those public-school playgrounds start sounding pretty great.

The route to getting our kids outdoors is not to throw away the computer or television set, no more than it is to throw away the books we have in our homes. These are all great sources of learning and enjoyment. Rather, the route is to make sure kids have real opportunities to play freely outdoors, with other kids, without interference from adults. Kids in today's world need to become highly skilled with computers, just as hunter-gatherer kids needed to become highly skilled with bows and arrows or digging sticks. To develop such skills, they need freedom and opportunity to play with computers, the primary tools of today. But for healthy development, they also need freedom and opportunity to play outdoors, away from the house, with other kids. The key words here are freedom and opportunity—not coercion.

Connecting to the natural world may simply become more challenging for young people as technology continues to improve, although augmented reality games like Pokémon Go offer an interesting exception. This is why summer camps, wilderness programs, forest schools, and other outdoor-focused organizations will continue to offer immense value to young people.

Connection to a Hopeful or Secure Future

Hari tells the story of one of his friends, a talented woman named Angela, who possessed a master's degree but nevertheless struggled to find work. Angela ended up taking an entry-level position at a London call center where she cold-called people asking for donations on behalf of British charities.

The call center operated with vicious efficiency. If Angela solicited successful donations, she got more shifts. If she failed to solicit enough donations, she got fewer shifts. Angela soon found herself barely earning enough money to get by, perpetually wondering if her next day would be her last. Cycling through phases of depression, anxiety, and anger, she even found herself envying her grandmother who long ago worked in London as a maid: a lowly position, but at least one with a stable annual contract.

Angela couldn't imagine a future for herself. She couldn't even imagine what next week would look like.

While writing this book, I was living in New Zealand where I became friends with a Spanish woman named Elena. Elena was in her late twenties, held a bachelor's degree, and had previously worked as a graphic designer before departing Spain for New Zealand on a "working holiday" to explore becoming a massage therapist. She soon found a position in the popular tourism town of Wanaka, where she had to be available for 10 hours a day for potential bookings. A new booking might arrive with only an hour's notice, but she only averaged two bookings a day. Elena loved massage but loathed the realities of working on-call; it "erased the feeling of being in control of my own life," as she told me. She quit soon thereafter.

Unfortunately, your kid may face this kind of workplace insecurity whether he likes it or not. As Hari explains:

> For the past thirty years, across almost all of the Western world, this kind of insecurity has been characterizing work for more and more people. Around 20 percent of people in the United States and Germany have no job contract, but instead have to work from shift to shift. . .By now, many middle-class people are working from task to task, without any contract or security. We give it a fancy name:

we call it being "self-employed," or the "gig economy"—as if we're all Kanye playing Madison Square Garden. For most of us, a stable sense of the future is dissolving, and we are told to see it as a form of liberation.

This isn't exactly cheery news, but I do see a silver lining in favor of unconventional education.

As the stable employment of the mid-twentieth century evolves into the gigs, projects, and self-employment of the twenty-first century, kids need to prepare for that reality. And how do you prepare a kid to embrace an entrepreneurial, uncertainty-riddled future? The first step seems clear to me: don't give them the false notion that there is a clearly defined path to success. Help them learn, through experience, that they must create opportunities for themselves.

In this regard, self-directed learning centers, radical alternative schools, and unschooling families do a wonderful job of modeling economic reality. Conventional schools tell students that if you play by the rules, economic rewards will automatically flow your way. This is still partially correct, of course, thanks to the signaling power of credentials. But such logic can also blindside young people like Angela and Elena who may have grown up thinking that high school plus college equals guaranteed security. Many mainstream educators now embrace "failure" as a buzzword—"let students learn through failure," they say—but it is the unconventional educators who truly put this concept into practice.

For many young people, life today is hard enough as it is. The journalist Susanna Schrobsdorff traveled the U.S. in 2016 talking with teens, parents, and professionals who work with teens. Here's what she witnessed:

> [Being] a teenager today is a draining full-time job that includes doing schoolwork, managing a social-media identity and fretting about career, climate change, sexism, racism—you name it. Every fight or slight is documented online for hours or days after the incident. It's exhausting.

There's no need to overwhelm your kid with the prospect of failure, but you shouldn't delude him, either. Take the middle path. Surround him with healthy peer groups, caring adults, and lots of opportunities. Let him play, improvise, explore the world, and grapple with boredom. Give him your unconditional love and support, without arbitrary deadlines. Give him as much control and responsibility over his education as he can handle, and as much freedom as you can handle.

That's everything you can do to connect your child to a hopeful and secure future.

In the End

How often do young people enjoy the social connections that support mental health? Surrounded by economic and social anxieties, watched by the all-seeing eye of social media, and squeezed by the academic pressure-cooker—is it any wonder that they're worried, disengaged, or depressed? Most are struggling just to keep their heads above water.

This is why places like Not Back to School Camp have the power to transform lives. They combine meaningful work, socializing, and values. They make everyone feel respected, they flatten social hierarchies, and they reconnect kids to nature. Most importantly, they give young people hope for the future.

When I was 14, I don't think I would have been ready for the closeness, vulnerability, and emotional intelligence of Not Back to School Camp. Luckily, I had another summer camp in my life—Deer Crossing Camp—that prioritized courage, proactivity, and outdoor stamina. Deer Crossing pushed me to grow in a way that school, family, or another camp probably never could have. (It also offered a lot of free time, which I mostly spent playing Magic: The Gathering with other kids in my tent.) Over four summers I developed a deep love for mountains, lakes, water sports, and wilderness backpacking. I banished my *T'naci* monsters. None of my camp friends lived close enough to became friends at home, but that was okay. Each summer at Deer Crossing was a world apart—one where I was valued, respected, and accepted. A world where I could recreate myself, over and over again.

Summer camps hold a special place in my heart, but all they represent is the possibility of meaningful connections. Maybe your kid will find her connections through sports, band, robotics, or a performing arts group. Maybe the spark will come through a voyage with Outward Bound, or a family trip abroad, or a local internship. Maybe your kid will come alive through an eSports tournament or attending VidCon. Or maybe, through their new alternative school or homeschool community, they'll make a handful of new friends—and that's all they'll need for a happy and healthy adolescence.

It doesn't matter, in the end, where the spark comes from. It only matters that your child's fire burns brightly.

Notes

For practical resources related to this chapter—and every other chapter in the book—please visit the book's dedicated webpage: https://blakeboles.com/y/

What I Learned at Not Back to School Camp

Grace and some of her long-term staff, I later discovered, were influenced by "Radical Honesty," a philosophy of direct communication, and "co-counseling," a reciprocal therapy practice emphasizing emotional honesty. Check-ins, in particular, were inspired by Grace's experience living in a communal house in college in which major decisions were made by full consensus.

The Kids Aren't Alright

On the many ways the world has been improving, see *Enlightenment Now* by Steven Pinker and "Ten Great Public Health Achievements—Worldwide, 2001–2010" (June 24, 2011). https://www.cdc.gov/mmwr/preview/mmwrhtml/mm6024a4.htm

The UCLA College Freshman Survey referenced can be found here: "The American Freshman: Fifty-Year Trends 1966–2015" https://www.heri.ucla.edu/monographs/50YearTrendsMonograph2016.pdf and here: "The American Freshman: National Norms Fall 2016" https://www.heri.ucla.edu/monographs/TheAmericanFreshman2016.pdf

For Twenge's quote about "5 to 8 times as many…" see "Birth cohort increases in psychopathology among young Americans, 1938-2007: A cross-temporal meta-analysis of the MMPI." in *Clinical Psychology Review* (2011). https://www.ncbi.nlm.nih.gov/pubmed/19945203. Twenge also looked for correlations between young people's mental health and disruptive historical events like economic recessions, mass unemployment, and wars. Even during the many disasters and disruptive periods of the 20th century, anxiety and depression rates were never as bad as they are today.

Twenge's summary of other research on the same topic: "Are Mental Health Issues On the Rise?" (October 12, 2015). https://www.psychologytoday.com/us/blog/our-changing-culture/201510/are-mental-health-issues-the-rise

"Between 2011 and 2015, a U.S. government survey reported a 50% jump in the number of teens demonstrating clinically diagnosable depression symptoms" is from "Why So Many Teens Today Have Become Depressed" by Jean Twenge (August 25, 2017). https://www.psychologytoday.com/us/blog/our-changing-culture/201708/why-so-many-teens-today-have-become-depressed. Note that these figures aren't simply an artifact of more teens seeking treatment.

"Another prominent survey of college undergraduates witnessed reports of 'overwhelming anxiety' jumping from 51% in 2011 to 63% in 2018" is sourced from the 2011 and 2018 ACHA-NCHA II reports: https://www.acha.org/documents/ncha/ACHA-NCHA-II_UNDERGRAD_ReferenceGroup_ExecutiveSummary_Spring2011.pdf and https://www.acha.org/documents/ncha/NCHA-II_Fall_2018_Undergraduate_Reference_Group_Executive_Summary.pdf

"The number of teenagers admitted to children's hospitals for thoughts of suicide or self-harm doubled between 2008 and 2015, with the majority of such incidents taking place during the school year" is from "Children's hospitals admissions for suicidal thoughts, actions double during past decade" (May 4, 2017). https://www.aappublications.org/news/2017/05/04/PASSuicide050417

Suicide rate for girls age 15 to 19 doubling between 2008-2015: "QuickStats: Suicide Rates for Teens Aged 15–19 Years, by Sex — United States, 1975–2015" (August 4, 2017). https://www.cdc.gov/mmwr/volumes/66/wr/mm6630a6.htm

Suicide rate for girls age 12 to 14 tripling between 2007-2015: "5 Reasons Why Self-Harm and Depression Have Tripled in Girls" by Jean Twenge (November 21, 2017). https://www.psychologytoday.com/us/blog/our-changing-culture/201711/5-reasons-why-self-harm-and-depression-have-tripled-in-girls

Teen happiness remaining high in recent decades: "Yes, Smartphones Are Destroying a Generation, But Not of Kids" by Alexandra Samuel (August 8, 2017). https://daily.jstor.org/yes-smartphones-are-destroying-a-generation-but-not-of-kids/. See also "Making iGen's Mental Health Issues Disappear" by Jean Twenge (August 31, 2017). https://www.psychologytoday.com/us/blog/our-changing-culture/201708/making-igens-mental-health-issues-disappear

Meet Johann Hari

All quotes and sources related to *Lost Connections* are from the book's first edition (2018). Note that Hari recognizes that today, few scientists still believe that depression is all about serotonin; the "biopsychosocial" model dominates the field. Also, on the list of connections, I chose not to include what Hari calls "connection to childhood trauma," as it felt outside the scope of this book.

Six Connections

Unless otherwise noted, arguments about these six connections and their purported effects on anxiety and/or depression are drawn from *Lost Connections*.

On the idea of building skills instead of following one's passion, see Cal Newport's 2012 book *So Good They Can't Ignore You*, as well as my critical review, "Is Following Your Passion a Bad Idea?" https://www.blakeboles.com/2016/03/book-review-so-good-they-cant-ignore-you/

For a forceful testament to the community-building power of online gaming, see Vicky Schaubert's article, "My disabled son's amazing gaming life in the

World of Warcraft" (February 7, 2019). https://www.bbc.com/news/disability-47064773

Peter Gray research on play and locus of control: "The Decline of Play and the Rise of Psychopathology in Children and Adolescents" in American Journal of Play (2011). https://www.psychologytoday.com/files/attachments/1195/ajp-decline-play-published.pdf

Susanna Schrobsdorff's quote is from "Teen Depression and Anxiety: Why the Kids Are Not Alright" (October 27, 2016). http://time.com/4547322/american-teens-anxious-depressed-overwhelmed/

CODA

In 2015 I traveled to the Upper West Side of New York City to visit John Taylor Gatto, the man who inspired me to take my first steps into the world of alternative education.

At age 80, John was bed-ridden, partially paralyzed by multiple strokes and type 2 diabetes. His wife Janet laid in the adjacent room, also bed-ridden with health issues. I shook hands with the Gattos' two home health aides, and then John and I settled into conversation.

John's speech was impaired by his strokes, but he patiently repeated himself and typed things for me on his computer as needed. He told me about the next book that he was about to publish—an illustrated children's book about a spider who works for the CIA—but mostly, John reflected on his time as an educator. He held fast to the principles that guided his earlier work: performance is more important than memorization; kids need real-world experience before they'll have an appetite for abstract academics; and one of my favorite Gatto-isms, "you need experience, adventure, and exploration more than you need algebra."

After an hour of conversation, John was tired. I thanked him, hugged him, and said goodbye.

That was the last time I ever saw John. He died three years later, in that same Upper West Side apartment, in the city that he loved—the city across which he helped so many young people adventure and explore.

When I think about John today, what stands out is his

unwavering faith in a young person's ability to know what's best for herself. John wasn't a naïve idealist in this regard; if his students were messing around or squandering opportunities, he would tell them so. But as far as I know, he never renounced his belief that "genius is as common as dirt" or that all people, young and old, are inherently worthy of freedom. Not freedom from pain, want, or worry, but rather, freedom from overreaching authority and unnecessarily wasted time.

After dedicating the better part of his life to teaching, John decided that conventional school hurts kids more than it helps. He spent his final years on earth promoting the small-scale alternatives that we've seen in this book: home-schooling, unschooling, democratic free schools, progressive schools, wild experiments within the public system, and everything in between.

School as we know it will probably be around a long time. Don't wait for it to change. If your kid doesn't belong there, then help them leave. On the other side of fear, a beautiful world awaits you.

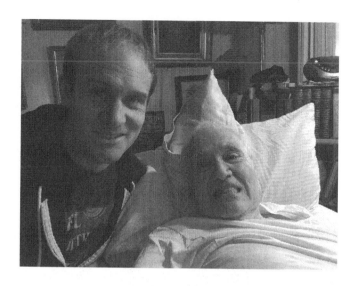

Blake and John, 2015

ACKNOWLEDGMENTS

Many people conspired to make this book possible. Ethan Mitchell helped turn a rough-and-tumble first draft into a self-respecting manuscript. Lori Walker, Kevin Currie-Knight, Joel Hammon, Wes Beach, Naomi Fisher, Brian Huskie, Kate Friedman, Danielle Denver, Tomis Parker, Nancy Tilton, Jon Lackman, Antonio Buehler, Jessica Rios, Peter Gray, Anna Smith, Gabe Cooper, David Martin, Margie Sanderson, Matt Sanderson, George Popham, Luba Vangelova, Ben Draper, Dev Carey, Ken Danford, Abram de Bruyn, Matthew Gioia, Madelyn Zins, Grace Llewellyn, Isaac Morehouse, and Bridget McNamer offered helpful feedback and corrections on a pre-publication draft. Kat Leeber, Maya Landers, Dan Moeller, and Stephanie Johnson were my trusty copyeditors and proofreaders. I'm indebted to Keiran Healy, Tom Ochwat, Kim Chin-Gibbons, Vanessa Reyes, Artec Durham, Amelia Bryan, Gavin Lake, and Jonah Meyer for sharing their personal stories. My 337 Kickstarter backers graciously helped fund my independent publishing costs with pre-orders, and my supporters on Patreon are absolute gems. "The Cell" in Wanaka, New Zealand, provided an ideal co-working space for shaping ideas into words. And thank you, mom and dad, for always believing in the path I chose.

ABOUT THE AUTHOR

Photo by Lauren Lindley

BLAKE BOLES is a writer, speaker, adventurer, and advocate for self-directed learning. He has spent more than a decade working with unconventionally educated teenagers through the trip-leading company he founded, Unschool Adventures. Originally from California, Blake has lived and traveled across the world. His previous books include *The Art of Self-Directed Learning*, *Better Than College*, and *College Without High School*, and his work has been featured in *The New York Times*, *The Christian Science Monitor*, *Psychology Today*, *Fox Business*, *USA Today*, NPR affiliate radio, and the blogs of *Wired* and *The Wall Street Journal*. He was born in 1982. Visit **blakeboles.com** to follow Blake's work and adventures.